RE-FORMING HISTORY

RE-FORMING HISTORY

*Mark Sandle and
William Van Arragon*

CASCADE *Books* • Eugene, Oregon

RE-FORMING HISTORY

Copyright © 2019 Mark Sandle and William Van Arragon. All rights reserved. Except for brief quotations in critical publications or reviews, no part of this book may be reproduced in any manner without prior written permission from the publisher. Write: Permissions, Wipf and Stock Publishers, 199 W. 8th Ave., Suite 3, Eugene, OR 97401.

Cascade Books
An Imprint of Wipf and Stock Publishers
199 W. 8th Ave., Suite 3
Eugene, OR 97401

www.wipfandstock.com

PAPERBACK ISBN: 978-1-4982-9998-5
HARDCOVER ISBN: 978-1-5326-0000-5
EBOOK ISBN: 978-1-4982-9999-2

Cataloguing-in-Publication data:

Names: Sandle, Mark, author. | Van Arragon, William, author.

Title: Re-forming history/ Mark Sandle and William Van Arragon.

Description: Eugene, OR: Cascade Books, 2019 | Includes bibliographical references and index.

Identifiers: ISBN 978-1-4982-9998-5 (paperback) | ISBN 978-1-5326-0000-5 (hardcover) | ISBN 978-1-4982-9999-2 (ebook)

Subjects: LCSH: History—Religious aspects—Christianity | History—Philosophy | Historiography

Classification: BR115.H5 S26 2019 (print) | BR115.H5 (ebook)

Manufactured in the U.S.A.   MAY 15, 2019

1. Scriptures taken from the Holy Bible, New International Version®, NIV®. Copyright © 1973, 1978, 1984, 2011 by Biblica, Inc.™ Used by permission of Zondervan. All rights reserved worldwide. www.zondervan.com. The "NIV" and "New International Version" are trademarks registered in the United States Patent and Trademark Office by Biblica, Inc.™

In Loving Memory of Kieran R. Otteson
(February 4 1997 – March 8 2019)

Rest in peace.

TABLE OF CONTENTS

Acknowledgments vii

Introduction: Beginnings 1

Chapter 1. Where Are We, and How Did We Get Here? 21

Chapter 2. Six Lessons from Johann Baptist Metz 39

Chapter 3. Reimagining Our "How": Re-Forming Our Practices 52

Chapter 4. The Power of Stories, the Wonder of Narrative 67

Chapter 5. Death of a Guardsman: *Hesed* and the Historian's Calling 89

Chapter 6. History That Heals 115

Conclusion. Endings, But Not an End 144

Bibliography 167

Name/Subject Index 175

Scripture Index 180

ACKNOWLEDGMENTS

We are grateful for ten years of enriching conversations with colleagues and students at the King's University. Thanks also to the wider community of Christian historians who have taught us much about the practice of history, and to the editors of *Fides et Historia*, the journal of the Conference on Faith and History, for permission to use and adapt previously published material.

We are grateful, most of all, to our families: Witty, Luke, Kim, Beth, Jacob, Caleb, and Sherlock (Mark); and Becky, Emma, Jon, Wink, and Sisko (William).

INTRODUCTION
Beginnings

We will start with an exercise of the imagination.

Imagine yourself standing around in the corridors of your history department for a moment. You look around and see two people that you have never seen before, strolling up to the front door of the building with some large sheets of paper in their hands. They begin to put the notices up on the doors. This is a defiantly radical act, for not only have the notices not been approved by the University Notices Approval Subcommittee, but they are also covering over the new university logo and slogan. A few people gather around, trying to see what is happening. The pair leave quietly. You go over, and start reading . . .

"*We offer the following theses as the starting-point for—hopefully—a long, contentious, and unsettling debate about History. So here are our 95 theses, pace Luther, to spark a discussion about Reforming History.*"

95 Theses

1. History is part of creation.
2. History matters.
3. History is too important to be left unreformed.
4. "History is that impossible thing; the attempt to give an account, with incomplete knowledge, of actions themselves undertaken with incomplete knowledge."[1]

---

1. Swift, *Waterland*, 94.

5. "History teaches us... to avoid illusion and make believe, to lay aside dreams, moonshine, cure-alls, wonder workings, pie-in-the-sky—to be realistic."[2]
6. Historians are united by a set of shared practices.
7. Historians are professional rememberers, and our disciplinary liturgies are practices of memory.
8. Historical inquiry and historical writing are recognitions of temporariness and impermanence.
9. The discipline of history is in crisis.
10. The discipline of history bears the imprint of the capitalist industrial modernity in which it exists.
11. The historical profession creates a reward structure which pushes historians to accumulate knowledge and use it for their own ends.
12. Professional history privileges white colonial narratives at the expense of stories from populations that have been suppressed and underrepresented.
13. Christian historians should start with this question: Who is my neighbor?
14. There are things Christian historians should not say and stories they should not tell.
15. More must be said to map out distinctively Christian liturgies and approaches to history.
16. Christian historians should do antihistory.
17. Christian historians should practice dangerous remembering.
18. The Christian historian must be driven by a partisan passion for justice—past, present, and future.
19. History must serve the living and the dead.
20. We must practice knowledge as love.
21. Christian historians should work to change history as agents of healing and hope.
22. Historians must guard against tendencies toward fragmentation and overspecialization.

2. Swift, *Waterland*, 94.

Introduction

23. Historians must avoid reductionism, generalization, lazy stereotyping, and unwarranted speculation.
24. There exist two terrible temptations at the heart of the professional identity of historians: to exercise knowledge as power over the dead, and to use the dead to pursue our own interests and ambitions.
25. The full meaning of history is not simply in what happened, but also in what did not or could not happen.
26. It is deeply inhuman to forget the dead.
27. Christian history must be rooted in the faith of hope within history.
28. "History as told from a place of invincibility is mostly about death. History told from a place of vulnerability is mostly about life."[3]
29. Historians should listen and care before they interpret.
30. Historians should seek wisdom, not originality.
31. Historians should seek advocacy, not utility.
32. Historians should seek healing, not explanation.
33. Historians should be seekers, not finders.
34. Christian history should move beyond modernity.
35. Historians should read lovingly.
36. Historians should read slowly.
37. Historians should be deliberately collaborative and collegial.
38. Historical practice should be based in love, not power.
39. History is endless.
40. History should lament.
41. History should console.
42. History must confront dangerous myths.
43. History must show that nothing is permanent, fixed, immutable.
44. History must help us to resist the allure of nostalgia.
45. Historians must work for others, not themselves.
46. We should be historians *sans frontieres* in a world without borders.

---

3. Peterson, *Christ Plays*, 151.

47. The responsibility of the historian is to help us all to live well and faithfully in the present and to peer hopefully into the future.
48. History should contest those voices which sing the siren song of progress at the expense of tradition.
49. History is strange.
50. History should make the familiar strange and the strange familiar.
51. Christian historians should listen to strange, unmodern Christian historians.
52. The historian should be an artist, a storyteller.
53. We need to narrow the gap between history and fiction.
54. Historians must concern themselves with the textural quality of the past; what it feels like, the threads and weaves and creases.
55. Historians work with the tension of trying to recreate the past and the urge to interpret it.
56. Historians must strive for an inventiveness of form.
57. History can be a spiritual discipline.
58. History can convert us.
59. History should serve life.
60. Historians should ask this question: What do we owe the dead?
61. Historians should brush against the grain of history.
62. Christian history is *Hesed*.
63. Historians should remove the cloak of invisibility from the stories of the marginalized.
64. Loving-kindness and care must be extended to all.
65. Historians should make the absent present.
66. Christian historians should write counterstories.
67. Historians should know when to be silent.
68. History is not neutral.
69. Christian historians should be peacemakers.
70. Christian historians must do justice, love mercy, and walk humbly with God.

Introduction

71. Christian historians should be ministers of reconciliation.
72. Historians must not play God.
73. Historians should resist all tyrannies equally.
74. Historical apologies must be accompanied by transformed social relationships.
75. There is no reconciliation without truth.
76. Storytelling and truth-telling are embedded in relationships, and some stories are not ours to tell.
77. Historians must not do epistemic injustice.
78. Historians must publicly contest those who deliberately and willfully seek to peddle lies, distortions, and half-truths about the past.
79. Christian historians should model unsettling pedagogies of history and hope.
80. Christian historians should practice Jubilee history.
81. History has always developed by both striking outward in search of the new and looking inward to renew.
82. The historian should tend to the past with love, care, mercy, and compassion.
83. Historians must cross the border between profession and vocation.
84. Historians must cross the border between the academy and the public sphere.
85. History should not be a private conversation within the academy.
86. Historians have a significant responsibility in building human solidarity across time and space.
87. Historians must tell stories about the universality of the human experience.
88. Historians must tell stories about the differences of the human experience.
89. History must reach out to recognize historic and systemic injustices.
90. Historians must be self-reflexive.
91. Historians must honor the historical record, the fragments of the past.
92. History should seek to stir us emotionally.

93. History knows that there are endings, but no end.

94. Christian historians must be sentinels of hope against the world's forgetfulness.

95. History can show us that another world is possible.

Re-Forming History

> Children, I always taught you that History has its uses, its serious purpose. I always taught you to accept the burden of our need to ask why. I taught you that there is never any end to that question, because as I once defined it for you (yes I confess a weakness for improvised definitions), history is that impossible thing; the attempt to give an account, with incomplete knowledge, of actions themselves undertaken with incomplete knowledge. So that it teaches us no short-cuts to Salvation, no recipe for a New World, only the dogged and patient art of making do. I taught you that by forever attempting to explain we may come, not to an Explanation, but to a knowledge of the limits of our power to explain. Yes, yes the past gets in the way; it trips us up, bogs us down; it complicates, makes difficult. But to ignore this is folly, because above all, what history teaches us is to avoid illusion and make believe, to lay aside dreams, moonshine, cure-alls, wonder workings, pie-in-the-sky—to be realistic.[4]

A Reformation?

We are writing this book in the context of the 500th anniversary commemorations of the beginning of the Protestant Reformation in 1517. Martin Luther's walk up to the door of the Wittenberg Cathedral to post his 95 Theses was an attempt to ask the church of his day to take a hard look at itself—at what it said, did, believed, and practiced. It proved to be a far more momentous act than Luther ever intended; inadvertently he started a religious revolution that changed the world. The 500th anniversary of the Reformation has prompted us to ask whether the discipline of history also needs re-forming (not that we expect to start a revolution or even be remembered in 2517 CE). Our aims are modest but still urgent: to contribute to the conversation among those Christians with a passionate interest

---

4. Swift, *Waterland*, 93–94.

Introduction

in the future of the past. What issues and questions about the discipline of history need addressing? How might we rethink, reform, renew, reimagine, and repractice the study of the past as historians or students of history? How might thinking about re-forming history shape what we do, how we do it, why we do it, and for whom? This short book is an attempt to engage some of those huge questions.

Using the Reformation as an imaginative point of departure, for better or worse, signals the fact that this is unapologetically a book written from a Christian perspective. We are historians at a small Christian university in Canada, and our approach is formed by our Christian convictions and Christian faith. While we invite anyone who is interested in the theory and practice of history into this conversation, we imagine that our readers will be Christian scholars, teachers, and especially students of history. In fact, we see students of history as our primary audience. As for the term "history," in this book we are speaking mainly of the type of history practiced in academic contexts, in colleges and universities in Canada and the United States (or the West more generally). Or, put differently, we are talking about the "historical profession" or "the discipline of history," which is only one of the myriad of ways that human beings, past and present, "do history." That said, we believe that the rich heritage of Christian theology and Christian scholarship can help us think critically, creatively, and imaginatively about the academic study of the past and help us to do it differently. This book is our offering on how to rethink the discipline of history and how to do history "Christianly."

Whatever Martin Luther intended, he did call for a turn in the church of his day. In the following pages, we will argue for what we are loosely calling a "theological turn" in Christian historical practice and scholarship. We acknowledge, however, that we are not theologians and that the voices we have chosen to guide us are selective and unsystematic. Readers will find no coherent "theology of history" here. We have tried to write for introductory history students and senior scholars alike, avoiding as much jargon as possible without over-flattening theoretical or theological ideas, terminology, and concepts. At times we will be intentionally forthright about our own theological and political convictions, recognizing that some Christian readers will not share them. So, like Martin Luther's 95 Theses (if we may be permitted the comparison), some may find our arguments to be banal, obvious, and conventional, while others may find them to be dangerous, subversive, or heretical. Either way, most historians of the Reformation now argue that whatever Luther's 95 Theses achieved, his original intention in posting them was simply to call for debate and discussion in the church about its practices. That is our goal, too, to ask for debate and discussion about how in this time and place we Christian students of history should practice our vocation faithfully and hopefully.

Why Now?

Why does history need a Reformation now? Let's start with the good news. History understood generally—and the accompanying sense of historical awareness or consciousness—has never been more popular. Historical novels, films, Twitter feeds, Broadway musicals, blog posts, documentary series, books, articles, and magazines are proliferating. You cannot escape this surge of interest in the past. Genealogical sites and resources allow people to plot their family histories, DNA testing has been harnessed and commercialized to trace our roots in the deeper past, and vacationers and tourists crowd historical destinations like monuments or theme parks by the thousands. Whether for idle curiosity or the need for entertainment or to fulfill some profound and essential human need, people love history. More narrowly, within the ranks of professional academic scholarship, history is also prospering. It has become a beautifully rich, diverse, and eclectic discipline. It has blossomed into myriad subfields, has explored all sorts of hitherto-unexplored fields of inquiry, has developed a range of new methodologies, and continues to grow by absorbing insights and ideas from other disciplines. Scholars continue to produce books and articles of incredible quality and in great quantities. Academic conferences on a variety of weird and wonderful topics abound. Thousands and thousands of students sign up to study history in universities and colleges across the globe. The past has never been more present in our consciousness than it is nowadays.

But ubiquity does not necessarily mean all is well, and popularity doesn't mean it cannot be done better, or differently. It just means that people are more aware than ever of the importance of the past to the present, and that human beings are captivated by stories of other human beings who lived in different times. Because if we peer below the surface for a moment, we will get a different picture. The historical moment we are in offers strong cultural and intellectual arguments for a conversation around reform. The times of crisis in which we live—postmodern, postindustrial, late capitalist, not to mention the existential threat of human-caused climate

Introduction

change—offer glimpses into a very different future for humanity. Now is a good time to stop and peer toward the new horizon that is beginning to hover into view. The highly unstable world in which we now live—riven by ethnic, racial, national, religious, gender, and cultural differences—presents a challenge for historians to consider the ways in which the past is (ab)used to fuel these conflicts, and how a different view of the past might help us to live well in the present.

In the cloistered world of professional historians there are problems aplenty. The general crisis situation in higher education—underfunding, resource shrinkage, increasing workloads around teaching, grading, and pressures to publish—is causing huge problems with morale and job security. All academic disciplines seem to be suffering from overspecialization, fragmentation, and overproduction. More and more is being published about less and less. The practice of professional history in universities cannot be divorced from this wider context. The pressures and tensions caused by the broader developments in the academic world have clearly affected the way history is practiced and taught. In Canada and the United States, too, professional history privileges white colonial narratives at the expense of stories from populations that have been suppressed and underrepresented. Simultaneously, the discipline of history, like others in the humanities or the liberal arts (literature, philosophy, theology, etc.), is increasingly seen by universities and society-at-large as unessential and irrelevant, not at all useful for training students for viable or "productive" careers. And universities in the West generally see students as customers to be served (and driven into debt) rather than full human beings to be nourished and loved. Is it possible to find a way of being and working that can counteract the drift toward overspecialization and fragmentation on the one hand, and the perception of irrelevance and uselessness on the other? How do we do history in a time of crisis?

Doing History "Christianly"?

As Graham Swift says in his amazing novel, *Waterland*, "History is that impossible thing; the attempt to give an account, with incomplete knowledge, of actions themselves undertaken with incomplete knowledge."[5] This sense of incompleteness, of the impossibility of history, is one that has been shared by countless reflective historians, past and present. What do we *do*,

5. Swift, *Waterland*, 94.

and what ideas and practices unite historians? Ludmilla Jordanova offers a simple and provocative answer to those questions in her book *History in Practice*. The discipline of history (or the profession), she says, is united by a *set of shared practices* rather than "a constellation of beliefs or theories, or a stable body of subject matter." Put simply, "History, the discipline, is about what historians do."[6] A more complex articulation of this idea that historians are what they do comes from Carolyn Steedman, whose 2001 book *Dust* is rich and suggestive for historians, and whose thinking has been very influential to us. She argues that professional historians "have to be less concerned with history as *stuff* . . . than as process, as ideation, imagining, remembering."[7] In a cryptic statement that tests the limits of our disciplinary empiricism, she tells us:

> Historians make the stuff (or Everything) of the past into a structure or event, a happening or a thing. What they write (create; force into being) was never actually *there*, once, in the first place. There is a double nothingness in the writing of history and in the analysis of it: it is about something that never did happen in the way it comes to be represented (the happening exists in the telling or the text); and it is made out of a past that *isn't there*, in an archive or anywhere else.[8]

That we make our history out of nothing is not a declaration of nihilism on her part; quite the contrary, in fact. It is instead a call to consider the ways we are constructed by our practices—or our *liturgies*—as historians, as professional rememberers, as storytellers, when we summon a past into being. How do our practices—our liturgies—define us, and how we do history? What might *Christian* liturgies look like?

If the discipline of history is based on a collective faith and trust in the practices or liturgies which sustain it, and if nothing is inherent in the stuff and the processes themselves, then we are not far from thinking about how those liturgies orient us toward the subjects we study and the audiences that we address. The term "liturgy" is a richly Christian one, of course, if we think of liturgies as the practices that shape our lives and our worship. As historians, we are, if you will, professional rememberers, and our disciplinary liturgies are practices of memory. Thinking about Christian faith and historical practice through the lens of liturgy invites us to think

---

6. Jordanova, *History in Practice*, 14.
7. Steedman, *Dust*, 67.
8. Steedman, *Dust*, 154.

Introduction

theologically about history, since after all, Christian faith (or faithfulness) is constituted or incarnated in memory practices, most centrally in the eucharistic sacrament. Christians, as the church, are people of memory. There has been something of a liturgical turn in Christian theology expressed by many scholars, including Christian philosopher and theologian James K. Smith. Smith defines liturgies as "rituals of ultimate concern" that form identity. "Liturgies are compressed, repeated, performed narratives that, over time, conscript us into the story they tell by showing, by performing." In Smith's phrase, we are "liturgical animals" whose fundamental longings and desires are shaped and formed by liturgical practices.[9]

And historians—Christians or not—have their liturgies. Thinking along such lines helps us as professional Christian historians to put our own practices under examination, to think about the liturgies that shape our discipline. Steedman, again, has observed that "Cognitively and rhetorically history-writing is constructed by an understanding that things are not over, [that] an Ending is not the same as an End. . . . Historical inquiry and historical writing are recognitions of temporariness and impermanence."[10] But if we read this from the perspective of Christian faith, we might also read the "End" liturgically. Smith has argued that human beings are "desiring agents,"[11] that we are what we love. Our identities are shaped less by what we believe, and more by the practices or liturgies that guide our hearts and direct our loves. As Christian historians, what do we love, and how should that shape our practices? What is the end of our remembering? Must Christian history look or be different than secular history? By no means do we intend to offer a normative template by which all Christian historians must measure themselves. There are as many ways for Christian historians to faithfully practice their craft as there are Christian historians. We do not claim to have final answers to these questions, but the questions, perhaps, are as important as the answers. And maybe the questions and answers will propose paths to re-forming history.

At this point we should introduce another observation about the current cultural climate in the historical profession. A foundational factor in our discussions in this book is that postmodernism has altered (or should alter) the terms by which historians understand the past. To paraphrase the title of a venerable Christian book on the subject, historical truth is

---

9. Smith, *Imagining the Kingdom*, 108.
10. Steedman, "About Ends," 99–114.
11. Smith, *Imagining the Kingdom*, 37.

stranger than it used to be.[12] For its many detractors, postmodernism—an amorphous and indefinable term that is associated broadly with poststructuralism, deconstruction, postcolonialism, the so-called "linguistic turn" and "cultural turn," and mystifying, inscrutable French philosophers—represents a clear and present danger to the integrity of the historical profession. Since the 1970s, according to its critics, the culture of postmodernism has cut against the authority of the discipline to describe historical reality. Reality, we are told, is essentially unrepresentable, thus there is no such thing as an authoritative or truthful version of any historical subject. The notion of a "turn" first came to prominence in the field of history with the application of the so-called linguistic turn (which argued that the past "does not exist outside our textual representations of it, and that these representations cannot be separated from the ideological baggage that historians bring to them."[13]). This was extended by the cultural turn (which looked to move away from the traditional concerns and sources of state politics, diplomacy, and economic indicators to explore how meaning can be found in the language of a culture or in its systems of representation), which has led history into lots of interesting and unexpected areas of inquiry.

We see in this current climate afforded by the emergence of poststructuralism, postmodernism, and the linguistic turn, an opportunity for re-formation—reconsidering how Christian historians pursue the past and relate to the discipline as a whole. To some, all these ideas seem to destroy the distinctiveness of history as a discipline. What makes the carefully researched product of historians a more authoritative source of knowledge about the past than, say, the latest Hollywood blockbuster? Even the most basic building block of historical research—the "fact"—is under assault. Where is the line between fact and fiction? If the past cannot be authentically described, what authority do historians have to offer moral judgments and lessons from the past? What is historical "truth"? Many historians, Christians included, see the product of postmodernism to be untenable moral relativism and nihilism, something to be opposed strenuously.[14]

We disagree, and we see in this current setting an opportunity for re-formation—reconsidering how Christian historians pursue the past and relate to the discipline as a whole. For its advocates, ourselves included,

12. Middleton and Walsh, *Truth is Stranger*.

13. See: http://www.history.ac.uk/makinghistory/themes/linguistic_turn.html

14. An excellent primer by an advocate of the uses of postmodernism in history is Callum Brown's *Postmodernism for Historians*. We have drawn from 1–11 and 158–59 in this paragraph.

INTRODUCTION

postmodernism is a liberative movement that throws open all sorts of possibilities about the languages of history and who can speak them. It lays bare structures of power and exclusion that had, under the banner of objectivity and neutrality, left out stories about women, gender, race, class, nature, and faith as being insignificant. Postmodernism has also been credited, rightly or wrongly, with creating new space for a generation of scholars to consider what Christian perspectives might mean for an understanding of the past. Christian historians are now much more free to consider what difference the "Christian" makes to their vocation. Having said that, we will not do much in this book to engage particular postmodern theorists and concepts except to suggest that this postmodern moment allows us to "move beyond modernity"—a phrase we will use frequently in the chapters that follow.

A "Theological Turn"?

Again, we are proposing a "theological turn" in the practices and writing of Christian history, and in doing so we are deliberately echoing opportunities and challenges offered by the postmodernist turn described briefly above. And although some readers may find that our approach to move beyond modernity will be maddeningly imprecise, it should be clear from the start that our use of the term "theological" is deliberately open and loose, and we will also occasionally use the words "sacred" and "spiritual" as synonyms to describe the turns we will outline for Christian practitioners of history to consider. Many people may be used to thinking of theology as a particular academic discipline, highly philosophical and learned in many contexts, with its own conventions and liturgies. But we use the term in a broader sense, more in line with how the late Ghanaian theologian Kwame Bediako defined theology. More than a rarified discipline, Bediako described theology as the "reflection about Christ that is carried on in the interface of the reading and hearing of the Scriptures and the experiencing of the actuality of Christ in the life situations in the world."[15] Theology, in other words, is rooted in, and is a reaction to, ordinary dilemmas to everyday reality—a reality that is sacred, because it is created by God—and asks the question, "How then shall we live?" We hope to consider how our practices ought to be turned theologically as we work in that part of God's creation we call history.

Furthermore, the idea of a turn—a move toward a different way of thinking and being and doing—is not new in history. The re-forming that

15. Bediako, "Doctrine of Christ," 110.

we propose is based on liturgies inspired by Christian theological insights and Christian worldviews. For reasons that are perhaps understandable, Christian historians in today's academy have been reluctant to apply interpretative models or perspectives from theology to their work. This fact has not gone unnoticed, and there are no doubt excellent reasons to be wary of joining too closely together two disciplines whose discursive interests are so different. The merging of theology and history runs the risk of veering into shallow moralism and insubstantial providentialism. There are things Christian historians should not say, of course. We should avoid the kind of providentialism that reads events (earthquakes, hurricanes, or terrorist attacks) as evidence of the hand of a judging God. We must not read events as the signs of times, or portents of some sacred calendar that is quickly and inexorably ticking to its fruition. But we should also avoid the opposite, a kind of functional agnosticism about God's presence and action in history where we profess that God acts in history but we do not see. We should consider ourselves free to revisit the riches of global Christian theological traditions which over two millennia of witness offer inestimable wisdom about history and time and how to do history. Today's Christian historians would do well to repossess and inhabit these traditions in order to derive alternative theories that might guide the practices by which we know the past.

The idea of a theological turn in the study of the past is both a very old idea and a new one at the same time. Theological insights about God and time and causality were at the heart of almost all the history that was written in the West prior to the eighteenth century. However, the idea of a modern theological turn in the writing of history is a relatively new one. Still, scholars are increasingly devoting attention to the place of theology in our understanding of the past. A recent roundtable at the 6th Annual Conference on US Intellectual History was devoted to exploring the place of theology in US intellectual history.[16] Historians there shared their sense that theology was occupying an increasingly important place in academic work, especially with the blurring of the sacred/secular divide, the growing critiques of secular modernity as a project from outside the West, and the increasing awareness of the importance of theological issues as motivations for human behavior. While this growing sense of the importance of theology in historical work has just started to come to the fore, this is not a new

---

16. The 6th Annual Conference of the US Society for Intellectual History, held on October 9–12, 2014 in Indiana, had a roundtable entitled "The Theological Turn in Intellectual History."

Introduction

development by any means. In particular, historians associated with the Conference on Faith and History have spent over forty years in the pages of its journal, *Fides et Historia,* debating precisely these issues.

One of these Christian historians, to whom we are deeply indebted, is George Marsden. Scholars like Marsden entered the historical profession in the 1960s and 1970s when overtly religious perspectives were viewed with antagonism. Over the years, Marsden has been the most prolific historian in defending the "outrageous idea of Christian scholarship."[17] If there is no such thing as scholarly neutrality and objectivity, he has argued, if all scholarship is perspectival, should not Christian perspectives be seen as valid as any others in the academy? An image that Marsden used frequently to define and defend a Christian worldview on history was a *gestalt* image.

FIGURE 1

[17]. For brevity's sake, our reflections in this introduction focus narrowly on George Marsden, whose arguments have been particularly influential for Christian historians in North America. As we will describe, the conversations on faith and history are much more diverse and wide-ranging than this. Marsden's principal writings on faith and history are: *A Christian View of History?* (1975); *The Outrageous Idea of Christian Scholarship* (1997); "Common Sense and the Spiritual Vision of History," (1984); and "What Difference Might Christian Perspectives Make?" (1998).

Look at the picture. What do you see: the young woman or the old woman? Or both? A Christian worldview, Marsden suggested, offers an extra set of lenses through which (figuratively speaking) the Christian scholar can perceive the deeper reality behind the surface of things. Marsden writes, "the epistemological implications of the Christian's knowledge of God are clarified" if we view them as "in one sense seeing everything differently than does the non-Christian, yet both of us seeing many of the identical things that are 'really there.'"[18] A Christian perspective on history is somehow additive in nature; we can see both and more.

For both of us, this analogy was, and remains, very useful and influential, but the inherent problems in this argument might also be readily apparent to some readers. Is there a singular Christian viewpoint or lens? Do Christians really see more than non-Christians? Does how they see make any difference for how they do history? Other Christian historians have, in fact, been very active in recent decades in theorizing answers to those questions. A helpful summary of the developments in Christian historiography over the last half century or so has been provided by Jay Green in his recent book, *Christian Historiography: Five Rival Versions* (2016).[19] Green has developed a fivefold typology for understanding different recent Christian approaches to understanding the past. The five are as follows.

One, Christian understandings of the past involve taking religion seriously. This includes religion as an object of study of people who lived at other times. Christian historians have been less likely to dismiss the power of religion, or dismiss it from historical analysis. In addition, religious commitments on the part of the historian enabled them to think and write with a certain type of empathy for, and identification with, those of that faith community. This hermeneutic of affection was simultaneously problematic but gave a certain type of insight.

Two (following Marsden), the use of a Christian worldview as a lens through which to view the world of the past. This lens on the past acts by bringing certain things into focus, and blurs other things. It can work in many different ways and is interpreted differently by different Christian scholars.

Three, the study of the past as an exercise in applied Christian ethics. Christian scholars should apply their Christian values to the study of the past, writing committed history, or value-laden history. In particular, this

---

18. Marsden, "Common Sense," 62.
19. Green, *Christian Historiography*.

approach denied one of the central aspects of the objectivity approach—the possibility and desirability of detachment—and instead argued for incorporating morality and moral insights into our accounts of the past. History thus becomes a form of moral philosophy, and moral instruction becomes one of the main purposes of studying the past: to help us live well in the present.

Four, historical study as Christian apologetic. In this approach, history is deployed as a means of defending the historicity of the Christian faith, affirming the historical basis for Christian belief, and outlining some of the ways in which the church has lived up to its mission over the years since the death of Christ.

Five, what Green calls historical study as the search for God, an attempt to craft a providentialist view of human history, which attempts to identify how human history fits into the broader story of salvation or redemptive history, a narrative centered on Creation—Fall—Redemption—Consummation.

Green concludes by talking about the need for Christian historians to recover a sense of vocation about their work, and to recognize what he calls the ordinary holiness of historical study. Carefully crafted historical study—marked by kindness, humility, and a commitment to truth-telling—is inherently valuable and desperately needed. Our work does not sit easily within the typology outlined by Green (it is perhaps closest to the third), but on this point we certainly concur, and this book is in part a response to Green's suggestion.

This book is driven by the conviction that more must be said to map out distinctively Christian approaches to history. We would suggest that Christian historians as a cohort still have work to do in imagining how faith shapes or ought to shape our practices as scholars.[20] Today, when Christian historians do avow their faith commitments or theological presuppositions in their work, these declarations usually take the form of introductory confessional or worldview statements but go no further. Thus the excellent question asked by William Katerberg: Is there such a thing as *Christian history*?[21] In other words, are there distinctively Christian hermeneutics

---

20. Christian historians in Canada and the United States have indeed been very active in theorizing the difference a Christian perspective makes, especially in *Fides et Historia*, the journal of the Conference on Faith and History. A recent collection of essays, *Confessing History*, edited by John Fea (2010), captures the best of this recent thinking, but also its limits.

21. See a series of essays in 2002 in *Fides et Historia*, esp. Wells, "Beyond 'Religious History,'" 41–47, and Katerberg, "Is There Such a Thing?," 57–66.

and practices evident in Christian history? Is Christian history *different*? Should we, or can we, say more about history? Is this a moment for re-forming history? We are animated by a number of strong convictions, especially around the ideas of hope, healing, suffering, justice, reconciliation, and solidarity in history. These convictions have led us to outline a number of key propositions which taken together constitute the central argument of this book.

A Map of the Book

It might be helpful for readers to imagine the sequence and structure of this book as circular, rather than sequential and linear. We ask readers to begin and end the book with our 95 theses, and the chapters that follow are thematic, drawing connections and echoes among them all. We begin in chapter 1 by taking a hard look at where history—as a discipline, as a profession, as a body of knowledge, as a community bound by a set of practices—is right now and briefly trace how we got here. We are trying to understand—using our Christian lenses—not just the surface issues, but also some of the deeper patterns and the longer trends at work in the movement of the academic study of the past. This will help us to identify some of the things which Christian historians should be thinking about when re-forming the practices of doing history.

In the following chapter we will argue that *Christian* history should take the prophetic mode of what we will call *antihistory*. We borrow this term from Catholic theologian Johann Baptist Metz and his emphasis on the dangerous memory of Christ's suffering as commemorated by the church in the Eucharist. Put much more simply, the Christian historian must be driven by a partisan passion for justice—past, present, and future. The next four chapters elaborate on these arguments further. In chapter 3, we will begin our critique of the profession and speculate on how and why we need to practice history differently. We will argue that we need to *look again* at our practices, at how we do what we do. We will argue for a set of practices centered on working slowly, lovingly, collegially, and incarnationally. Wrapped up in this discussion will be the need for historians to recover a sense of vocation—the purpose for which the past is being studied—to underpin all our activity. In chapter 4, we will look at the power of story and narrative when we consider how we should tell the past. This means firstly a need to *look back* and recover the former ways of talking about the past,

Introduction

as derived from the Christian and other traditions which existed before the professionalization of the discipline, and consider what we might have lost that could be fruitfully recovered. Secondly, we need to *look around* at how others tell stories. By looking at how the past can be told, we will emphasize the importance of story, creativity, and imagination in history.

Chapter 5 starts with what we propose as one of the fundamental questions that all historians must address: What are our responsibilities to other humans, both the living and the dead? We argue that history needs a new ethic (or set of ethics) to underpin it, and that this can best be summarized as history that serves both the living and the dead. This chapter unpacks the idea of *Hesed* (drawn from the Jewish/Old Testament tradition) which argues that a posture of loving-kindness toward the dead is the highest form of kindness as it cannot be reciprocated. As the work of the historian is concerned overwhelmingly with dead human beings, then an ethic of loving-kindness toward the dead should shape and inform all that we do. And in chapter 6 we argue that our historical practices must be concerned with change, with the future, and with justice. This chapter contains an analysis of, and reaction to, Canada's recently completed Truth and Reconciliation Commission (2007–2014), which addressed the fraught colonial history between settler Canadians and Indigenous peoples. Using the TRC as a point of departure, we will argue for immersive, engaged, and future-oriented Christian historical practices that contribute to healing, justice, and reconciliation. Instead of adopting a posture of scholarly detachment or assuming that our task is simply to describe the past as it really happened, Christian historians might instead work to *change* history as agents of healing and hope. Finally, we will return to the beginning to conclude by revisiting the 95 theses that opened this book, and set out some of the central ideas we have about history from a Christian perspective.

This is a book, then, written for anyone who is interested in the practices of history and Christian faith, and what the two have to do with one another. It is directed especially toward any student of history who might be interested in the relationship of Christian belief to the study and understanding of the past. As practicing historians who are also Christians, we also hope this book will encourage readers to investigate further the rich scholarship by Christian thinkers and historians who also have explored the ways in which their faith affects how they see that part of God's creation we call history. We see this book as an invitation to a conversation, not the final word on the subject, and along the way we hope to inspire and edify—and perhaps provoke, perplex, and annoy—our readers. If this book does nothing but incite our audience to read and think more deeply about what our Christian faith means to understanding and studying the past, even if that response is motivated by disagreement or irritation, we will be pleased. We hope what you read will provoke you, cause you to pause, reflect, and think a little more about what it means to do history and be a historian, and make you then go and do likewise.

CHAPTER 1

WHERE ARE WE, AND HOW DID WE GET HERE?

"Learning from the past is a great idea that is almost never taken seriously."[1]

Does History Have a Problem?

As we said in the introduction, Ludmilla Jordanova argues that history is best understood as a set of *shared practices*, rather than any core knowledge. So what are these practices and processes that together constitute what one might term the "liturgies" of the discipline? What we will do in this chapter is briefly examine the development of these liturgies, or these practices and rules that guide our doing of history, and offer some explanation of where these rules came from. If we are to fruitfully rethink the discipline, we need to be aware of the ways in which how we do what we do have been formed. We began this book with the premise that the discipline of history is in crisis. There are issues within the discipline itself that all historical practitioners either experience or recognize, and these things seem to be calling out for a change in how we do history. Four major issues or areas of tension stand out.

1. Bendroth, *Spiritual Practice of Remembering*, 7.

Competition and Collaboration:

The current landscape within which historians work is a deeply ambivalent, almost paradoxical one. The system displays both competition and rivalry but also deep cooperation and collegiality. Practiced and portrayed as an artisanal craft, it actually operates with a deeply industrial ethos. Profoundly individualized, it nevertheless requires collective efforts to function properly. In some contexts it is radically subversive, while in others the discipline serves the interests of the powerful.

(Most) historians are rooted in two separate but related communities: the university and the disciplinary community. In the university, the historian competes for resources, status, promotion, increments, grants, and rewards to further their career. In both the classroom and in their research, the university historian appears as an autonomous agent, seeking career advancement (or job security), tenure, and so on. But the historian is also part of a wider community: the disciplinary community. This community can be seen as acting a little like a guild: a semi-closed organization, governed by a particular set of norms, values, ethics, and practices, fiercely protective of its interests. (Major examples of these guilds include the American Historical Association and the Canadian Historical Association.) Once it begins to coalesce, the system reproduces itself and expands. More and more historians take their place in the guild, competing with one another yet at the same time preserving the system. Historians train undergraduate and graduate students in their ways, and they rise up and join the ranks, perpetuating the essential practices. At the heart of this guild lies a deeply contradictory set of pressures. As in the university, the first of these is an ethos of competition—competing for grants, jobs, esteem, and publishing contracts. But again, the guild is also a place of deep human interaction, creativity, and collaboration. Historians work closely together to improve each other's work, encourage and inspire one another to seek out new ways of thinking about things, collaborate on research, read manuscripts, and comment on conference papers. The guild operates to foster competition and collaboration and creativity, but it also produces conformity, which is also partly why many of the key developments in historical methodology and practice have come from outside the guild. The discipline of history has been one of the most active borrowers of interpretive theories and practices from other fields, for example from the social sciences and literary theory.

Where Are We, and How Did We Get Here?

Truth, Skepticism, and the Objectivity Impasse

Postmodernism, for example, is one of those disciplinary imports, emerging first from fields like literature, literary theory, linguistics, and philosophy, and it has altered the terms by which historians understand the past. Since the 1970s, according to its critics, the culture of postmodernism has cut against the authority of the discipline to describe historical reality because there can be no essential distinction between fact and fiction, between history and invention. History, many have said, must be defended against such heresies. This essential and deep-seated skepticism about the validity of historical knowledge, the credibility of the discipline, and the knowability of the past has created something of a crisis for practitioners of traditional history. Where do they go from here?

Perhaps the most contentious (but by no means the only) recent debate since the arrival of postmodernism has been about the possibility and/or desirability of objectivity in the writing and researching of the past. As Christian historian William Katerberg has noted, today the debate has reached something of an impasse.[2] The twentieth century began with a fairly widespread acceptance that the heroic model of objectivity from the natural sciences—the lone, detached, autonomous, objective scientist who has the God's-eye view and is able to transcend their own culture and background and beliefs—could be more or less replicated in the study of human society. Gradually, of course, this came under attack; first, from the recognition of the inescapable subjectivity of all human scholarly practices, and second, because science itself came to be seen as no longer a neutral activity, but as something deeply shaped by politics, ideology, or commerce.

As the discipline of history retreated from the heroic model of objectivity, it decided to circle its wagons around a more limited understanding of objectivity, one marked by communal group accountability and disciplinary conventions. Under the shadow of increasing skepticism unleashed by postmodernism, Katerberg argues that

> it is noteworthy that in recent decades the project of defending objectivity in which the professional institutions and methods of the discipline provide checks and balances that keep scholarship honest, and the diverse, contentious and (ideally) democratic community of scholars judges which scholarship is reliable, even if controversial, and which is unreliable. This pragmatic objectivity is grounded institutionally, culturally, socially and indeed

2. Katerberg, "'Objectivity Question,'" 101–27.

politically, and is not heroically transcendent or individually autonomous. The knowledge produced is thus universally valid only insofar as it is judged so by a diverse community of scholars in a given time. And it is stable and reliable rather than completely relative, because some points of view are ruled out of bounds.[3]

This pragmatic idea of objectivity has been reinforced by other developments, including the linguistic turn, which argues that language is all that we have in trying to understand the past. We only have the traces left behind by the past—words to look at, hold, decipher, translate, and try to make sense of. We have no direct access to the people of the past, thus the traces produce profound limitations on our ability to know the past, which go beyond our inherent human subjectivity.

Some historians—while still retaining the pragmatic, diluted understanding of objectivity—retreated further, arguing either that the pursuit of historical truth and objectivity was in itself a worthy activity (even if objectivity itself was an illusion and unattainable), or that perhaps an approach rooted in subjectivity and empathy was more valuable. But most historians acknowledged the impasse between those who argued that objectivity was impossible and that history had to change how it worked, and those who argued that history was provisional, limited, and contingent. And so we reached an impasse. No one accepted the old heroic model of objectivity any more. No one was really sure whether or not the word was useful anymore: Should it be retained but redefined, or abandoned? Was it something you pursued, but would never attain? No one could agree on whether history itself was impossible, or whether the discipline could just carry on, but more circumspectly and less confidently.

The impasse dragged on. And everyone just went quietly back to work.

History as Industrial Era Activity

The discipline of history is increasingly coming to bear the imprint of the capitalist industrial modernity in which it exists. The scale of the production of history—the manufacturing output of historians, as it were—is profoundly affecting not just the quantity of history being produced, but also the type of history, and the way in which research is carried out. The pressures to publish or perish in higher education mean that history is being produced in unheard-of quantities: more and more research, more

---

3. Katerberg, "Objectivity Question," 103.

and more books and scholarly journals, more and more articles, more and more conferences, more and more television documentaries. And more and more historians are taking up positions as the global expansion of post-secondary education continues apace. So what lies behind these pressures to publish?

The expansion of history has created competition among historians both to acquire jobs and to get promotion and tenure. This requires publishing consistently, and publishing in a field where no one has published before, as this marks you out as an original and outstanding scholar. Thus, the quest for originality in research and to publish it are the key markers of success for the historian. In this increasingly competitive landscape, the response of the historian looking for originality has been to specialize, and to greatly increase their output of published works. Specialization enables historians to pursue originality because producing knowledge about this or that niche area demonstrates tangibly that they are one of the leading experts in that particular field. Historians increasingly are forced to become specialists of smaller and smaller areas (or topics or periods or themes). The output—the book or article or research grant—then acquires value for the historian, as it becomes a commodity which can be used to secure the job, the promotion, the tenure, or the improved status or reputation. This constant search for originality—new sources, new interpretations, reinterpretations, new ways of understanding the past—and the ever-expanding production of historical knowledge through books, conferences, articles, and so on, are all a deep expression of the way history has been gripped by an industrial-type ethos: accumulate, specialize, produce, commodify, exchange. History is produced in vaster and vaster quantities, for ever-increasing markets for consumption by readers, viewers, bloggers, and students.

The drive to expand the output of history has also had an impact upon the research techniques and practices which are used to produce this work. In particular, the need to produce published material as quickly as possible—so its benefits can be quickly reaped—has created a utilitarian approach to reading, research, work with the sources. It is like the extraction of mineral resources. The sources have to be mined, the information dug out of them as quickly and as efficiently as possible, so that it can be processed and manufactured into valuable commodities. The research process then becomes something deeply utilitarian, governed by the need to produce the desired output.

FIGURE 2

FIGURE 3

What does this mean for history at present? Overall this has led to fragmentation, overproduction, and homogenization within the discipline, with more and more people becoming specialists in smaller and smaller areas. This makes it difficult for the community of historians to speak and converse with each other. Specialization has not on the whole been accompanied by increasing numbers of works of synthesis which seek to reconstitute the bigger picture, although there are some notable exceptions.

It also appears to be the case that we have a crisis of overproduction: Is anyone reading all of this output? More and more work, which is increasingly highly specialized in its focus, is being published, but hardly being read by anyone. At the other end of the spectrum, much to the disgruntlement of ordinary professional historians, you have highly popular works of history in the public sphere (books, films, and TV) being consumed in vast quantities. But these are increasingly focused on a few highly popular topics: war (especially World War II), the Nazis, dictators, and biographies. Popular history has become homogenized (with one or two notable exceptions) by the diktat of the market and the drive of commerce, ratings, and sales. Like the homogenization that consumerism has produced in our modern Western retail spaces, popular history defaults to a few key topics, personalities, events, and time periods. So we have this dichotomous life of history: academic history of minute, fragmented specializations which are largely unconsumed (the work produced by the backstreet artisans), and the popular history of Hollywood, the History Channel, and airport books (the mass-produced work), which is consumed in vast quantities.

History as Profession

Finally, the processes of professionalization and becoming a professional discipline have left their imprint upon the practice and ethos of the study of the past and in turn created a set of pressures to act and work in particular ways. Because it is set within a career structure, the profession creates a reward structure—tenure, promotion, publications, prestige—which pushes historians to accumulate knowledge and *use it for their own ends*. This instrumentalist attitude toward knowledge becomes by extension a utilitarian attitude toward the people of the past. When we use knowledge to support our scholarly ambitions, we are in effect using the people—the defenseless dead—for our own purposes. There thus exists two terrible temptations at the heart of the professional identity of historians: to exercise knowledge as power over the dead, and to use the dead to pursue our own interests and ambitions.

But, how did we get here?

Becoming History

What is history today? And how did it get to be like this? The discipline of history as we practice it in the West has long roots, but our very short account of the profession's current liturgies and practices goes back about 400 to 500 years. Three things stand out. Firstly, history developed an empirical methodology to ensure its reliability. Secondly, history became a professional discipline. Thirdly, history became an eclectic, diverse discipline, defined in the main by a commitment to a set of shared practices.

Becoming Reliable: History as Empirical Knowledge

History developed in tandem with the broad Western intellectual trends of the sixteenth, seventeenth, and eighteenth centuries, especially the Reformation, the scientific revolution, and the Enlightenment. Prior to the eighteenth century, as David Lowenthal puts it, "History's great truths were received and eternal: the Historian's mission was not to find them but to buttress preconceived conclusions such as the existence of God."[4] With the Enlightenment came a diminishing faith in received truth and the wisdom of tradition. Instead, the judgment of the individual historians in establishing historical truth became more pronounced. The Enlightenment's faith in the ability of human reason to understand what was wrong with society and then to try and fix it led to a stress on useful knowledge that could help change things. A better future could be ensured if we could only analyze the human experience more fully and more clearly. Knowledge for its own sake was no longer prized. The utility of knowledge to help humanity make the world better, fairer, and more just and humane, was increasingly seen as its core value.

But this raised another question: How do you generate reliable knowledge? In science, this began to be addressed in a general sense by the rise of the experiment as a legitimate way to make knowledge. Starting from the premise that humans could only really know that which they had made for themselves, they began to see the experimental method as key to producing reliable, useful knowledge. Truth had to be testable, able to be confirmed or verified. And this experimentalism could only be relied upon if there were correctly identified rules and methods which had been established and were practiced rigorously. This stress on following the right rules and

---

4. Lowenthal, *Past is a Foreign Country*, 343.

Where Are We, and How Did We Get Here?

procedures arose as a response to the problem of producing reliable knowledge, free of passion, distortion, bias, and emotion. This meant trying to be detached, distant, and dispassionate in their work. The combination of these things—the drive for useful knowledge, the growing popularity of the experimental method, and the striving for detachment—created a strong impulse in favor of empirically based studies in many fields of human inquiry.[5]

So how did this impact history? Around 1800 and after, history started to think of itself as a discipline which sought to accumulate knowledge about the past so that it could be used to help us understand the present. In addition, it also began to define a methodology for itself which fell in line with the experimental method in the sciences. This pushed history toward a preference for primary over secondary sources (for here the historian could have direct experience of the past and thus manufacture their own knowledge), and this in turn privileged archival work and also contributed to the development of series of practices—including critical reading and objective writing—which were also designed to guarantee its impartiality. The historian had to try and remove as much bias and partisanship as possible from their work. Historians thus were coming to realize that the credibility of their discipline rested on their ability to demonstrate their methodological rigor and expertise in the process of accumulating knowledge about the past.[6]

What emerged was the empirical method. Anna Green and Kathleen Troup have helpfully summarized this method, the core tenets of scientific empirical history, as follows:

- the rigorous examination and knowledge of historical evidence, verified by references;
- impartial research, devoid of *a priori* beliefs and prejudices;
- and an inductive method of reasoning, from the particular to the general.[7]

Implicit within these research principles is a specific theory of knowledge, first of all, that the past exists independently of the individual's mind, and is both observable and verifiable. Secondly, through adherence to the

---

5. Appleby et al, *Telling the Truth about History*. See esp. chap. 2.
6. Brown, *Postmodernism for Historians*, chap. 1.
7. Green and Troup, *Houses of History*, 3.

research principles above, the historian is able to represent the past objectively and accurately. In other words, the truth of a historical account rests upon its correspondence to the facts.[8]

The emergence of this essentially empirical approach to history evolved primarily out of the German school of scientific history in the mid-nineteenth century.[9] The dictum to reconstruct the past "as it essentially was" also coincided with the expansion of the modern state's drive to collect their archives of key government documents and treaties. In this way, the archival approach was born, as historians sought out the documents which would enable them to "tell it as it was." Empiricist approaches argue that careful work with the original or primary sources will enable us to produce accurate, reliable knowledge about the past, but nothing more. These accounts will always be a "partial sketch of a vanished past." This type of work is cumulative, collective, and open to refutation. It builds on the work of others, engages with the work of others, and is open to better, more accurate views of the past coming along. Thorough, detailed work within the archives is central to the work of the historian, according to this view. Gradually a methodology emerged, peculiar to history, as practitioners refined and developed their techniques for understanding these archival materials.

So, scientific experimental methodology pushed historians to develop rules and methods to establish its credibility, reliability, impartiality, and objectivity. It also communicated the idea that the archives were the place, and the primary sources the raw materials, for their work—their laboratory, if you like. Reliable knowledge about the past could be produced as a result of immersion in these sources and the practice of these methodological rules.

Becoming Professional: History as Discipline

The story is incomplete, however, without looking at how history emerged as a fully-fledged professional discipline after 1800, and how it evolved and expanded between the mid-nineteenth century and today.[10] Professional history emerged out of this broad intellectual, cultural, social, and political milieu. The drive to professionalize the discipline came from its own

---

8. Green and Troup, *Houses of History*, 3.
9. Feldner, "New Scientificity in Historical Writing," 3–21.
10. Lambert, "Professionalization and Institutionalization of History," 40–60.

practitioners. Historians sought out a professional status for themselves in order that they might begin to occupy an authoritative position in terms of who could and could not legitimately and reliably interpret the past. As historians began to acquire the status of professionals within the expansion of university learning in the nineteenth century, so they became recognized as those whom society relied upon to tell us what happened and why. The foundations of this authority rested on their claims to objectivity, linked to methodological rigor, archival research, critical reading, and the like. In doing this, the historians started to distinguish themselves from historical novelists and purveyors of historical fiction.[11] Instead they focused on pursuing the model of scientific detachment, and the methods and skills associated with this. These skills became a way of identifying what it was that marked out historians from other people who write about the past or who made other claims to authority over the past. These liturgies and practices were fixed to the discipline's claims to a kind of cultural authority relative to other ways of knowing the past. They learned these skills, and then they passed them on to others.

But this required an institutional setting for it to take place: resources, physical space, and a context for controlling the process and providing career structures to allow access to the profession and to moderate and develop it. This was the university. And so, alongside professionalization there also developed the processes of institutionalization. As university education grew after 1815, history increased in popularity. Partly this was a response to the emergence of new nation-states in Europe (as these states looked to create a founding myth for their past and historians were pressed into service), and partly this was the work of academic entrepreneurs who took the opportunity to develop new courses as part of the competitive drive to recruit more students. In countries like Germany, Belgium, and France, universities began to create new history departments, focusing upon primary source archival research, critical analysis, and the research seminar. History as a discipline expanded rapidly after this. It became linked strongly to the project of nation-building and national identity, whilst also moving out across national boundaries, moving from Europe to North America, and then latterly to South America, Asia, and Africa.[12] This geographical expansion has been accompanied by both a numerical

---

11. Lowenthal, *Past is a Foreign Country*, chap. 8.
12. Lambert, "Professionalization and Institutionalization of History," 44–54.

proliferation and also (particularly since World War Two) a massive growth in the range of topics and sources that historians have shown an interest in.

The one constant in the last 150 years of expansion and development has been this commitment amongst professional historians to these practices and methods in order to produce reliable, useful knowledge about the past. The production of reliable knowledge is significant in two ways. One, if it is not accepted by the rest of the historical community, then it cannot produce the outcome the historian wishes—promotion or tenure or recognition or reputation enhancement or being published—and thus lacks value. Two, it continues to reinforce the authority and professional status of historians *in toto*. Being recognized as the group that provides a society with its history affirms their professional status and their authority as the legitimate interpreters of the past. This highlights the way in which these shared practices operate. Accuracy and reliability are prized for their apparent ability to get us closer to the truth about "how the past really was" or "what happened" and indeed "why it happened." But these methodologies are also deeply self-serving (for historians or organizations or governments or publishers): they produce knowledge which can be used (and abused), deployed, and commodified. They protect the group.

Becoming Modern: Expansion and Consolidation of History

The professionalization of history has been accompanied by two things: a rapid and massive expansion of the discipline, and a growing sense of a commitment to a set of shared practices as the main thing which unites all historians. As we saw above, history is incredibly diverse and eclectic in terms of what people choose to research and write about, the sources they use, the frameworks they deploy, and the ways in which they make their research publicly available. From the German scientific school of the nineteenth century has emerged a bewildering variety of forms of history: the *Annales* School, a spectrum of Marxist types of history, political history, intellectual history, social history, gender history, postcolonial history, and cultural history. Histories which borrow from anthropology, sociology, and statistics. Micro-history, oral history, history of material culture, Big History, counter-factual history, and future history.[13] Accompanying this

13. A number of works trace the history of the discipline itself. See: Green and Troup, *Houses of History*; Marwick, *New Nature of History*, esp. chaps. 3 and 4; Hoefferle, *Essential Historiography Reader*.

diversification of interests and the pluralization of approaches has been a massive increase in the number of historians and the amount of history being done. Across all continents, history has expanded to become this prominent feature of modern life: in our public spaces, in movie theatres, in online spaces, in our thinking, in our shopping malls, and in our bookstores. It is truly ubiquitous.

While all working historians have a particular, narrow field of research (and a broader set of teaching interests), what unites most historians working today are their efforts to know, understand, or make sense of the past by engaging with the traces left behind by the past. The origins of the discipline in its modern form lay in developing and codifying a set of practices and methods which dealt with the problems of working with sources located in archives. These practices developed, really, as a form of problem-solving. These solutions then became codified into a process with a concomitant set of practices and questions. But without understanding the problems, it is rather difficult to make sense of the practices. The essential problem that historians set out to solve was how to get the traces (the primary sources) left behind to talk so that they could give us solid, reliable information with which to write our histories. Our knowledge about the past had to be accurate if it was to be used, or if it was to be considered reliable. Hence the stress on developing the right methods and practices—in the search for truth—and an emphasis on the historian being as detached and objective as possible, free of passion, bias, or subjectivity.[14]

Let's dig a little deeper though, and ask two further questions. One: What do historians think they are doing?

As a set of practices, the discipline of history developed a mode of working, a process that has the following stages or sequences:

- Reading around the subject in general and identifying key questions, problems, lines to pursue
- Finding/locating the empirical traces that the past has left behind
- Appraising these traces carefully and then making inferences as to the most likely meaning of those traces
- Arranging, collating, verifying, and organizing the resultant material

---

14. See, for example, Marwick, *New Nature of History*.

- Turning this material into an end-product of some description, such as a book, article, magazine, blog post, film, or TV documentary[15]

This process is fairly well established (although the first two points often happen simultaneously) and so the process is not necessarily sequential. Often it is more dynamic and complicated than that. At a deeper level though, this process is guided by different assumptions according to what the historians believe they are doing. When historians begin this process of finding the traces and end it by producing some knowledge about the past, there appear to be roughly four different positions as to what this process is trying to achieve. These types can be broadly categorized (and these are rather crude generalizations) as reconstructionists, empiricists, constructionists, and deconstructionists.[16]

Reconstructionists might be viewed as the most optimistic of these groupings. In what might be termed its "crude" or "naïve" form perhaps, the reconstructionist position is that historians can reconstruct what really happened to a greater or lesser extent: the traces—if they are handled correctly—can give us a realistic sense of what was going on in the past. This is related to the historicist ideal, which outlined that the goal was to show what actually happened. Hence the idea of reconstructing or recreating what happened. To be sure, hardly any historians occupy this position any more.

Empiricist approaches differ from those of the reconstructionists by arguing that the idea of reconstruction, or recreating the past, is impossible. Instead they argue that careful work with the sources will enable us to produce accurate, reliable knowledge about the past, but nothing more. These accounts will always be a "partial sketch of a vanished past."[17] This type of work is cumulative, collective, and open to refutation. It builds on the work of others, engages with the work of others, and is open to other better, more accurate views of the past coming along. Its claims are more modest than those of the reconstructionists, but it shares a concern with careful work with the traces as being central to the work of the historian.[18]

Constructionists attempt to synthesize elements of the empirical approach with the use of theories and concepts derived from the social

---

15. For example, see the helpful introductory work, Storey and Jones, *Writing History*.

16. Munslow, *New History*, 1–23. See also Furay and Salevouris, *Methods and Skills of History*.

17. Furay and Salevouris, *Methods and Skills of History*, 14.

18. Brown, *Postmodernism for Historians*, chap. 1.

sciences. Here, the emphasis falls very much upon the use of theory and concepts to try and uncover the deeper meanings or underlying patterns at work in human history. In particular, these approaches tend to highlight the processes of historical change at work: Why, and how, do things change? The empirical dimension is crucial as well, though; it should not be seen as secondary since it is primarily deployed to reinforce that analytical framework. In this way, the history is constructed by the historian, using the raw materials of the past (the traces), but also with blueprints (ideas, concepts, structures, theories) supplied by other people in other times. Most historians would see themselves as either empiricists or constructionists (or a combination of the two).

Deconstructionists stand at the other end of the spectrum from the reconstructionists. In its most radical incarnation, deconstructionism outlines that history is merely a literary activity, which amounts to nothing more than a representation of the past. History is a creative act of the historian. It is a new thing entirely, a third thing in fact, meaning that there is no essential difference between history and fiction or between primary and secondary sources. The first thing is the past (which does not exist). The second thing is the traces (which do exist). The third thing is the literary output which historians write, which is a completely new thing, a representation of the past. This is not a position held by most professional historians, although it is gaining ground.[19]

Most historians working today, in our estimation, occupy the empiricist/constructionist part of this spectrum. What unites these approaches, however, is that the problem of knowing, or making sense of, the past has in some way to be done by working with the traces left behind by the past. This is why it is so important for all historians—and those training to be historians—to reflect upon these methods.

At the heart of these practices are a series of questions which guide the work of the historian with the traces the past leaves behind. It is sometimes remarked upon that getting the traces to speak is a little like interrogating a rather reluctant witness in a court case. It is something that requires patience, skill, empathy, and the instinct to ask the right questions. We have broken down these general questions into two separate parts: external and internal. These have become a litany or catechism for all practicing historians.[20]

19. Munslow, *New History*.
20. These can be found in most history methodology textbooks. See, for example,

External Criticism:

- When was the trace produced? How close to the events? Can it be accurately dated? Is it authentic?
- What type of trace is it?
- How did it come into existence and for what purpose?
- Who created it?
- To whom is it addressed?
- How reliable is the creator? Were they in a good position to provide first-hand information?

Internal Criticism:

- What was happening at the time?
- What does it say?
- Is there bias that must be accounted for?
- How was it understood by contemporaries?
- Can the details be corroborated?
- Do the events/actions/words seem likely/probable/realistic?
- What does it mean, then?[21]

In this way, history came to be defined as a set of practices shaped by these questions—rather than a core body of knowledge—which inevitably meant creating some consensus amongst historians as to what these might be.

What do these practices tell us about history and historians? A few things, actually. One, the overriding concern for historians is for truth and accuracy, not necessarily as ends in themselves, but so that their accounts can be considered reliable. Most historians would argue that their histories need to be derived from, and rooted in, an honest reading of the traces or sources. Two, a stance of scholarly detachment is most conducive to a

---

Marwick, *New Nature*; Furay and Salevouris, *Methods and Skills of History*; Tosh, *Pursuit of History*.

21. There are of course various supplementary questions and approaches we need for different types of primary sources: oral history, material elements, cartoons, or photographs, and so on.

reliable account being told. Three, an accurate account of the past can be unlocked if the right practices are pursued with sufficient diligence and consistency. Four, the central part of scholarly work is analysis and critique of the materials that you read, and the safest approach is to adopt an attitude of intense skepticism to anything that you handle. Five, the overall approach of the profession should be the accumulation of as much knowledge as possible from the archives. This will then be critiqued, evaluated, and interpreted. Six, the work of interpretation is never finished, and so all conclusions are contingent and open to revision. Seven, the job of the historian is to analyze, explain, and understand—not to judge.

In sum, history and the work of the historian is about:

- accumulation of knowledge
- accuracy and reliability
- analysis and interpretation
- detachment and skepticism
- revisions

It is a cumulative process of progressively increasing knowledge and progressively increasing interpretative dispute and debate in which we seem to know more and more, yet understand less and less.

Two: What do historians value above all, and what does this tell us? Many things spring to mind. Here are a few of the most obvious ones:

- Publications (especially books and above all the research monograph—not for the financial rewards, obviously, but for the prestige, the sense of peer acknowledgement, the idea of being "the" expert in the field)
- Originality (being the first to find that document or advance that new interpretation)
- Time spent working in the archives (so you can complete your book or find that never-before-seen document)
- Time spent writing (to complete the publication)
- Going to conferences (to listen to other ideas and views in your field, to network about jobs or mutual research interests)
- Money to do research (to enable you to do all of the above)

- Time spent with students (PhD, MA, and undergraduate students, in that order)

In sum, the historian is concerned with output and productivity: publishing original work, and preferably doing it as quickly as possible. To achieve this, the work is often done at breakneck speed. Ironically enough, time (or the lack of it) is perhaps the greatest enemy of the historian. Publications must be done quickly (to get tenure, or to meet the deadline imposed by the publisher, or to be the first into print with your thesis). As we saw earlier, the fusion of time, competition, originality creates enormously strong pressures toward specialization, fragmentation, and overproduction.

So, history has evolved and expanded in tandem with the broader social and intellectual currents of industrial modernity, and also the internal dynamics of the discipline itself, as practitioners have explored the boundaries of the discipline and reflected upon how to refine and enhance these methodologies. The fabric of modernist history is woven from three strands of cloth in particular: a source-based empirical methodology, professionalization/institutionalization, and specialization. The processes of professionalization and institutionalization—set in motion at the start of the nineteenth century—have themselves created a set of self-supporting and self-sustaining pressures which have shaped the discipline. History carries in itself the imprint of these three elements, and problems are starting to appear as we noted above.

The time is right to re-form our study of the past, we believe. But how? Where should we start??

CHAPTER 2

SIX LESSONS FROM JOHANN BAPTIST METZ

So far, we have argued, the historical profession is in crisis and our methodologies and practices are similarly skewed. So what do we do? The next few chapters lay out some suggestions for how we might re-form and reanimate our liturgies as Christian historians. This short chapter sets the stage by introducing the concept of Christian *antihistory*, a term that may sound forbidding and adversarial at first. And perhaps it is. This idea comes from German Catholic theologian Johann Baptist Metz, and there are several purposes for unpacking it in this chapter. We offer this brief introduction to Metz's thought as an example of the ways in which theology can influence and direct the practice of history, and how it can provide insights into renewed historical liturgies based on sacred practices. We will examine the notion of *Christian* history as *antihistory* or *dangerous memory*, concepts which are derived from Metz's work. We do so to begin asking what a historically minded theologian might have to say to theologically minded Christian historians about the *practice* of history. We are proposing that Christian history ought somehow to be different—why embark on the project of Christian history otherwise? As asked by William Katerberg, the conversation revolves around this question: Is there such thing as *Christian* history?[1] In other words, are there distinctively or peculiarly Christian practices evident in the work of Christian historians? Is Christian history *different*—ontologically, ethically, aesthetically, ideologically?[2] Do

---
1. Katerberg, "Is There Such a Thing," 57–66.
2. Katerberg suggests that the Christian historian might turn profitably to the theology of the incarnation. Perhaps "Christians ought to start with the question: 'Who is my

Re-Forming History

Christian historians know something about the past that non-Christian historians don't? Do they do history differently? How should it be different?

One theologian whose work offers a guide to doing Christian history differently is Metz. We will begin to simply introduce his work and ideas by deriving six lessons from his life and thought, especially circling around his concepts of "antihistory" and "dangerous memory."[3] Some of what follows might be rather dense and theoretical, but it's important for the overall argument, and we will be as clear as we can.

Lesson One: History is Rooted in Relationships

We shall start biographically, as Metz often does when explaining his ideas, by describing two events in Metz's early years. These episodes, he would later confess, were particularly formative in the conception and development of his political theology, and his concepts of antihistory and dangerous memory. The autobiographical element, Metz has said, is central to this theology; what happened to him affected and shaped his thought. What we want to illustrate through Metz's example is how we must center our very selves—our own biographies and stories—in our practices of history. History is inherently relational, and we must always remember that there is a vital and sacred connection between our lives and experiences as historians and those human beings we study: the living dead.

Metz grew up in Nazi Germany. In 1945, during the final stages of Germany's defeat in World War II, the sixteen-year-old Metz was forced out of school and conscripted into the German army, and after some brief training he and about 100 other ill-prepared youths were sent to the front. One evening, Metz was sent alone to deliver a message to the army headquarters. He got lost, and wandered all night long through an apocalyptic landscape, past destroyed, burning villages and farms. When he returned to his company, he found that all his friends and comrades had been killed in an Allied attack. "I could see only dead and empty faces," he wrote, "where the day before I had shared childhood fears and youthful laughter. I remember nothing but a wordless cry." This cry, Metz later thought, and the memory of those faces of his dead friends, opened a fissure in his life and

---

neighbor?'" This is a moral imperative and a postmodern question, not one "seeking the closure of objective knowledge, but the indefinite, endless obligations of citizenship, both human and divine" ("Is There Such a Thing," 66).

3. Our understanding of Johan Baptist Metz's theology is based particularly on his writings and on Morrill, *Anamnesis as Dangerous Memory*, especially chaps. 2, 4, and 5.

shattered his youthful Christian assumptions and optimism.[4] This was the first great trauma of his life, one that he continued to place at the center of his theology. What did the deaths of his friends mean? What did it mean to keep their memories alive as he himself continued to live?

Perhaps unsurprisingly, the second fissure or great trauma in Metz's biography, as he calls it, is the reality and memory of Auschwitz. Like many postwar German intellectuals, Metz's work shows the shadow of the Holocaust and reflects questions about German guilt for the genocide. Yet he constantly protests against views of the Holocaust that would somehow place it outside the reach of human analysis or comprehension, as inscrutable, beyond words, or beyond interpretation. Auschwitz, Metz has said, "has profoundly lowered the threshold of shame between human beings,"[5] but the suffering was personal and human, as were the actions of those who perpetrated it. As a German Christian and a member of the perpetrating culture, Metz needed time to grapple with this crime, and by his own admission it was not until the 1960s that Metz was able to compose a coherent post-Auschwitz theology. To this day, Metz remains troubled by his failure as a theological student soon after the war to visit the concentration camp at Flossenberg, where Dietrich Bonhoeffer was murdered.[6] In the end, where many saw in Auschwitz the death of God, Metz concluded otherwise: "we can pray *after* Auschwitz, because people prayed *in* Auschwitz."[7]

In short, Metz's theology began from personal experiences—deeply painful ones—and was rooted in relationships between himself and those he remembered. In imagining the meaning of the suffering of his lost friends, and of the Jews murdered in Auschwitz, he realized that all his theological scholarship was tied to real people and embedded in human relationships, regardless of whether or not those people were still alive. There is a sacred insight here, one we will elaborate on later in the book. While our own experiences as people and historians are profoundly different, the useful point of connection is the recognition that our life experiences and relationships are an essential part of the history we do. In fact, there is something deeply inhuman in the modernist historical liturgies that tell us that we need to remain neutral and detached both from our own biases and from the subjects we study. How can we stand apart from those we are called to love?

4. Metz, "On the Biographical Itinerary," 2.
5. Schuster and Boschert-Kimmig, *Hope against Hope*, 17.
6. Schuster and Boschert-Kimmig, *Hope against Hope*, 15–16.
7. Metz, *Emergent Church*, 19.

Lesson Two: History as Antihistory or Dangerous Memory

For Metz, the memory of these Second World War events represented formative, shocking interruptions in the life of this theologian for whom history and memory became such crucial concerns. In a body of work stretching over four decades, Metz has made memory one of the crucial concepts of his political theology. What is the historical and theological meaning of suffering? How ought we to remember the past Christianly? These are essential questions for Metz, and for us as Christian historians.

The act of genuine Christian remembering, writes Metz, is dangerous. It can be dangerous and subversive because it "threatens the present and calls it into question because it remembers a future that is still outstanding."[8] For Metz, nothing expresses the church's "dangerous memory" more than the central sacrament of the church, the Eucharist, a rite that subverts the world's realities because the knowledge that what God has done in human history through Christ's death and resurrection is a shocking and threatening interruption to all notions of progress, as well as a source of forward-looking hope for Christians to work for a world made new. The Christian story of salvation and redemption is dangerous because it is the real story, the real history we live in, whether or not the world recognizes it.

Most fully expressed in Metz's 1977 work *Faith in History and Society*, and amplified in countless other books and papers, "dangerous memory" encapsulates Metz's view that the task of theology today must be essentially practical and subversive. Here it is useful to reference the twentieth-century philosopher and cultural theorist Walter Benjamin, from whom Metz derived the term. "Articulating the past historically does not mean recognizing it 'the way it really was,'" Benjamin wrote in 1940. "It means appropriating a memory as it flashes up in a moment of danger. . . . The danger threatens both the content of the tradition and those who inherit it."[9] Metz seizes on the threatening flash of memory and places it at the core of his theological project. He argues that "the Church must understand and justify itself as the public witness and bearer of the tradition of dangerous memory of freedom in the 'systems' of our emancipative society."[10] A Christian sacramental remembering of history that we glimpse and practice in

---

8. Metz, *Faith in History and Society*, 200.

9. Benjamin, "On the Concept of History," 391.

10. Metz, *Faith in History and Society*, 89–90. All quotes are from this edition, but a newer edition also exists: J. Matthew Ashley, editor and translator (New York: Crossroads, 2007).

the Eucharist, in other words, is a freeing reminder of the real truth of history that somehow liberates us from false narratives of the past, present, and future. Here he cautions us that "the God of this dangerous memory does not secretly become a political utopia of universal liberation."[11] Metz is equally distrustful of the teleological certainties of Western liberal capitalism *and* Marxism (and, indeed, any ideological teleologies), all of which, he argues, are undergirded by notions of a secular utopian redemptive future.[12]

Memory, then, refers to "the fundamental form of expression of Christian faith and [to] the central and special importance of freedom in that faith." In this faith, Christians hold to the testament of Christ's love, incarnation, suffering, and resurrection. By remembering Christ's suffering and sacrifice, the church "is liberated from all attempts to idolize cosmic and political powers and make them absolute." Dangerous remembering as a baseline from sacramental historical practices thus supersedes modernist history as something more than a screen for today's secular ideologies and interests. It is from this sacramental and incarnational premise, Metz tells us, that the church "can and must draw its strength to criticize all totalitarian systems of government and all ideologies of a linear and one-dimensional emancipation."[13] This is inherently dangerous, Metz tells us, because the church's memories, liturgies, and hopes are not the world's.

Metz's emphasis on the dangerous memory of the suffering of Christ and the church is tied inextricably to his injunction that we remember also the victims of history, those who have suffered and/or been forgotten. But with this premise, Metz intends something more far-reaching and subversive than post-event restorative justice, processes of truth-telling, reconciliation, and forgiveness—although these are certainly essential, and we will discuss these in a later chapter. Our idea of history, Metz argues, is distorted by the screening out of the importance of suffering. We tend to view history in almost a Darwinian sense as the history of what and who has prevailed through struggle. Simply put, we focus on the winners

---

11 Metz, *Faith in History and Society*, 67.

12. Two contextual points are worth mentioning here. First, Metz's theology is/was clearly positioned as a response to Cold War ideological struggles, which he, as a German Catholic, felt so keenly. Second, Metz's affinity for and indebtedness to Latin American liberation theology is clearly evident, as his political theology seeks to encompass the polycentric realities of world Christianity, a church divided between the emergent church of the global South and the bourgeois church of the West. See especially Metz, *Emergent Church*, 1–16.

13. Summary and quotes from Metz, *Faith in History*, 89–91.

of history, and we give no meaning or credence to the losers—in fact, we deliberately forget them. Christian antihistory inverts this assumption. "It is of decisive importance," says Metz, "that a kind of *antihistory* should develop out of the memory of suffering—an understanding of history in which the vanquished and destroyed alternatives would also be taken into account." The memory of supposedly futile, meaningless suffering in the world, Metz concludes, "cancels all affirmative ontology and all teleology as untrue, and exposes them as a mythology of modern times."[14] To put it much more simply, the real meaning of history is found with the losers, not the winners.

Lesson Three: Remembering the Dead

From this kind of sacramental counterfactualism or antihistory, Metz is able to offer a definition of sacred history as that form of "world history in which the vanquished and forgotten possibilities of human existence that we call 'death' are allowed a meaning that is not cancelled or recalled by the future course of history."[15] The full meaning of history, if you will, is not simply in what happened but also in what did not or could not happen. But the memory of past suffering can only be meaningful when it is connected to the recovery of particular *subjects* in the human story. Metz's model is the Old and New Testament narratives in which men and women are "constituted as subjects through their *relationship* with God."[16] The covenantal and relational aspect of memory is crucial. By remembering the victims of the past we are also remembering (dare we say reincarnating?) them. "It is deeply inhuman to forget the dead," Metz tells us, because forgetfulness "is an acceptance of the meaninglessness of their sufferings."[17]

The subversive potential of Christian antihistory, the recovery of the subject through dangerous memory, is, we would suggest, one of the most appealing dimensions of Metz's historical imagination. How can we as Christian historians move beyond modernity? How can we do history that honors the dead? How can (or should) we remember dangerously? Perhaps this ethical orientation does not constitute the basis for any new or significant methodological distinctives for Christian historians. But let

---

14. Metz, "Future in the Memory," 3–16; quotes 9.
15. Metz, "Future in the Memory," 12.
16. Metz, *Faith in History and Society*, 61.
17. Metz, *Faith in History and Society*, 75.

us briefly offer some possible implications of what this practice of dangerous Christian remembering might look like before embarking on a more fulsome exposition in the next chapters of what differences it might make.

Lesson Four: History is Telling Stories

On the face of things, the idea that history is telling stories is banal and obvious. That's what historians have always said they do, and so there are no claims to originality here. But how do we tell stories? What relationships are we placing ourselves in when we tell them, or when we listen? Who do our stories serve? Ourselves? The powerful? We never do history from a position of neutrality, so all our practices are in the service of something or someone. Who then shall we serve?

The first point is that Metz's arguments offer a critique of the historian's conventional genre and methodology itself. Whatever manner of change that postmodernism has occasioned in our discipline, at bottom the academic historian's methodology remains rooted in modernism—it is evidentiary, positivist, empiricist. For better and worse, we Christian historians who labor in the academy must play by the rules of our profession. But Metz places memory and narrative as improvements over "historical reconstruction." We need "narration against time," he says; "we must try again and again to tell stories." We should create a narrative culture through which "a coalition between those who are alive today and those who have died, been forgotten, sacrificed, or vanquished in the past" will be formed. A scientific, modernist kind of history without the incarnational narrative cannot produce or open up those connections between the present and the past, or link the suffering church across time and space as fellow image bearers of God.[18] It cannot suffer with the forgotten, the dispossessed. Nor can it make us open to the gravity of the moral claims of the dangerous memory of the past. It cannot chasten us or even convert us. We should, in other words, remember sacramentally, just as we repeatedly recall Christ's suffering in the Eucharist.

Another implication of Metz's theology, we think, is to invoke and practice the prophetic ethos inherent in Christian dangerous remembering in a manner that is necessarily practical and political. As the remembered history of suffering, Christian history-making might reclaim the subversive form of dangerous tradition. All forms of colonialism and imperialism,

---

18. Schuster and Boschert-Kimmig, *Hope against Hope*, 30.

Metz argues, are based on the destruction of memory. The enslavement and colonization of peoples begins when their memories of the past are taken away or when their histories are delegitimized. Recovering the memories of past suffering, in other words, is inherently subversive. In Metz's phrase, these memories are "like dangerous and incalculable visitants from the past," and as they haunt us they also undermine our social, political, and cultural certainties.[19] Or, to quote the title of theologian Stanley Hauerwas and William Willimon's important book, these are memories that hold us to our identity as "resident aliens" in this world.[20] They are subversive challenges to the empires of our day.

Lesson Five: Dangerous Memory and Justice

The relationship here between dangerous memory, ethics, and doing justice is probably evident, since the capacity to remember correctly seems imperative to ongoing processes of seeking justice, reconciliation, and forgiveness, or as a collective response to genocide and atrocity. Two writers, Mary Grey and Dermot Lane, have reflected on the ethics of dangerous memory in a volume honoring two Latin American archbishops and liberation theologians, Oscar Romero of El Salvador and Juan Gerardi of Guatemala, who were among the hundreds of thousands of people brutally murdered during those countries' civil wars.[21] What, they ask, is the Christian duty to the memory of those who have died and who obviously can no longer speak for themselves? Lane takes up Walter Benjamin's injunction on the openness of the past, arguing that history "is a form of empathetic memory. What science has settled, empathetic memory can modify."[22] With this as his premise, Lane declares, "In virtue of the . . . solidarity that exists within the human family and in light of the empathy of the human heart with the sufferings of the victims of history, humanity has an ethical duty to remember."[23] In terms of Christian witness, remembering the victims of historical injustices is a keenly prophetic act—an act of justice—interrupting the existence or appearance of continuous, homogenous, meaningless time by hearkening to the action of God in time through Christ's crucifixion.

19. Metz, "Future in the Memory," 12.

20. See Hauerwas and Willimon, *Resident Aliens*.

21. This volume is a collection of essays and recollections: Hayes and Tombs, *Truth and Memory*.

22. Benjamin, quoted in Lane, "Memory in the Service," 176.

23. Lane, "Memory in the Service," 180.

Memory does not inevitably lead to justice and reconciliation, but it is a necessary step toward reconciliation and forgiveness, since the alternative, allowing the wounds of history to fester, can create "a hereditary disease" which can further perpetrate recrimination and retribution.[24]

Mary Grey amplifies these themes in an essay that describes her vision for what she calls "a theology for the bearers of dangerous memory." In Grey's usage, dangerous memory has a transformative and subversive potential. By remembering the victims and sufferers of history, Christians collectively have the opportunity to radically reshape unjust social relations and to emancipate those still trapped by them. This collaborative response to atrocity, past and present, is inherently subversive since "the bearers of dangerous memory are keeping alive the very core of Jesus' project of the Kingdom of God, which of its essence must conflict with the wisdom of the kingdoms of this world."[25] The duty of dangerous remembering is work that requires a radical form of empathy, and as such it is an exercise in profound humility for those engaged in it. Grey explains, "To stand with the memory of the 'crucified peoples' of the world is only possible within a continual conversion experience in which we are dependent on the generosity of the peoples themselves for forgiveness."[26] The nexus between memory and forgiveness, and between victim and advocate, must be enacted in theology and faith communities where Christians will hear, honor, and bear witness.[27] Against the world's dangerous and threatening amnesia, in other words, the church must stand with resolute, active remembering. So must Christian historians, we would argue.

Lesson Six: Holding Hope within History

The dominant mood of these essays, which echo Metz's concepts of dangerous memory and antihistory, is one of hope, of passionate optimism about the restorative, prophetic, and healing power of memory. But most professional historians in North America, Christian or otherwise, do not labor in conditions of particular danger. However, Metz, Lane, and Grey place into relief ideas about memory, justice, belief, and reconciliation in ways that are useful. Furthermore, they collectively link into ongoing

---

24. Lane, "Memory in the Service," 190–92.
25. Grey, "Theology for the Bearers," 165.
26. Grey, "Theology for the Bearers," 165.
27. Grey, "Theology for the Bearers," 162.

conversations among theologians of liturgy. Consider how the sacraments summon up and embody God's presence in human time and so create and perpetuate Christian community across space and time. In effect, by remembering Christ's crucifixion in the Eucharist we are also remembering him (although we are exceedingly conscious that some Christians see this as literal and others as metaphorical or analogical remembering). "Liturgy is that collective memory of the Church . . . and that memory's centre is the Eucharist," argues Jesuit writer Wendelin Koster.[28] The Eucharist stirs the memory in two ways, according to Peter Atkins. First, it draws to mind linkages and associations between the sacramental elements and the death of Christ. Second, it links past, present, and future in a single fold, recognizing that Christ is part of history and foreshadowing his coming again.[29]

Other theologians extend the point by reclaiming the eschatological dimension of the Eucharist, since it is a meal celebrated in hope and anticipation of the promised kingdom of God. According to William Crockett, this perspective—and here we are right back to ethics—is clearly linked to the theme of justice. "A meal celebrated in prospect of the coming reign of God must give rise to a new social vision grounded in the promise of the kingdom," he declares. The Eucharist is a memorial of hope, and to make a memorial of Christ's death and resurrection is to actualize it prophetically in the present and in doing so to bind up together a new community; it is inherently subversive and liberative because it questions the foundations of present society.[30] This, again, is the kernel of Johann Baptist Metz's concept of dangerous memory.

And hope is the key. Christian history must be rooted in the conviction of hope *within* history. Any Christian theology, Metz argues, can be defined as a defense of hope in the God of the living and the dead.[31] What if Christian history did likewise? A Christian view of history implicitly subverts all merely secular ideologies whose ends lead away from God. "History as told from the place of invincibility is mostly about death," writes Eugene Peterson. "History as told from the place of vulnerability is mostly

---

28. Koster, "Recovering Collective Memory," 32. His essay reflects an anthropological turn in studies of liturgy, drawing on the idea of worship as performance and marking out the repetitive, cyclical, and rehearsed nature of worship as memory.

29. Atkins, *Memory and Liturgy*.

30. Crockett, *Eucharist*, 256.

31. Metz, *Faith in History and Society*, 3.

about life."³² Like Christ our teacher, we vote for life-giving history instead, and for vulnerability. A life-giving Christian vision of history is about more than suffering; it must also be about consolation, hope, and reconciliation. And that hope must be found within history itself, otherwise history is meaningless. It is very easy to see hope and beauty in nature; anyone can look at a beautiful mountain scene and imagine that a benevolent Creator is behind it all. It is more difficult to scroll through history—which seems so predominantly tragic—and come to the same conclusion. Yet history, too, is part of creation. Should it not command in us awe and wonder, the same assurance of God's presence, as any other facet of creation?

We hope the reader will assume our answer is an emphatic "yes," and it is; and we see it as central to any cultivation of Christian antihistory or dangerous memory. But our argument in support of this contention will be rather impressionistic. For an illustration, please consider the map below:

FIGURE 4

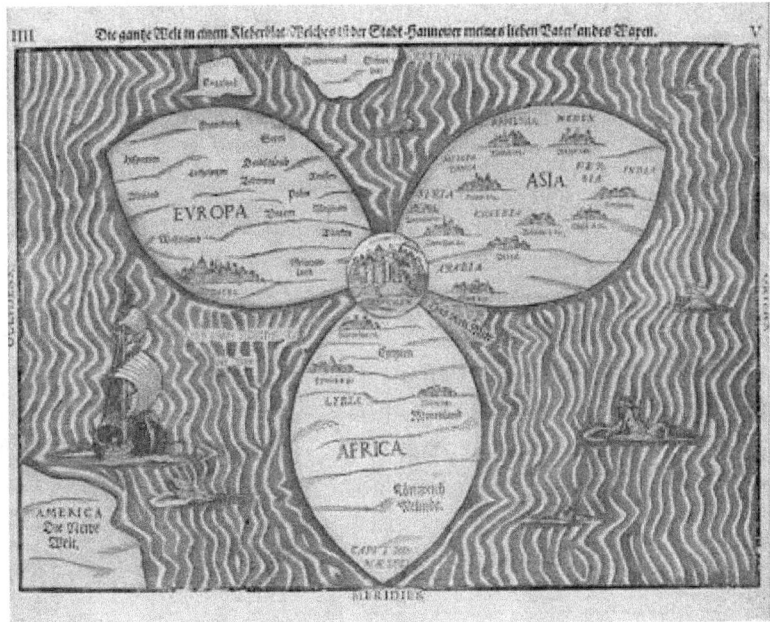

32. Peterson, *Christ Plays*, 151.

Re-Forming History

This map, from 1581, is by the German cartographer Heinrich Bunting (1545–1606). It will be readily apparent that the map's usefulness as a conveyor of accurate geographical information is rather limited. It shows us the world in the form of a cloverleaf, each continent proportional in size, reflecting the order and harmony of the cosmos. There are hints of disorder, too: America lurks forebodingly in the bottom corner as if presaging the shock of modernity, and England, as usual, has stubbornly refused to join Europe. In the center, of course, is Jerusalem.

This map is more than a metaphorical depiction of geographical space; it is also a figure of historical time. Western historical thinking since St. Augustine has been linear in orientation; St. Augustine saw human history as essentially a subplot in the divine and unfolding story of the city of God, and there is a long tradition of Christian thinkers since then who have read the human story as a linear narrative which ends in God's redemption of all things. Since the Enlightenment, Augustine's vision of the coming city of God has been replaced with visions of secular redemptive futures (to use Metz's term). History is directional and purposive, and time is the metric by which history is measured. As Christians, then, we know the end of the story; we know that history is not "but a brief crack of light between two eternities of darkness."[33] We believe that history is about life and not death, and that the meaning of history is found somehow not outside of time itself, but is within history, within time, because God is present with us. History is not a morgue, because the tomb is empty.

Bunting's map gives spatial and temporal expression to an undervalued term that is resonant of a more sacramental and Christian understanding of history: the fullness of time. Creation, fall, and redemption are telescoped in space at Jerusalem; linear time is shot through with eternity. Christ's incarnation and resurrection—the hope of history, the hub around which the world spins—is as immediate and present to us now as it was to his disciples. Christian historians would do well to think of time in its fullness rather than its pastness. Theologians from liturgical traditions—Catholic, Anglican, Orthodox—are much more accustomed to reading history in this way, to seeing God's presence as embodied in the church across time and space and recalling Christ's resurrection as both past and immediately present. "That one divine action [Christ's resurrection] is both a set of historical events and an eternal act, the self-giving of the Son to the Father in the Trinity," writes Anglican theologian Rowan Williams. "The

---

33. Nabokov, *Speak, Memory*, 19.

life of Jesus is in its entirety a working out in time of an eternal relation of adoration and love."[34] Ecclesiastes 3:11 says "God has set eternity in the human heart"; God has also set it in the center of time—past time and our time simultaneously. "Whatever is has already been, and what will be has been before,"[35] and here we think of the incarnated and resurrected Christ, that alpha and omega from which flows God's adoration and love.

The implications of this, however, are not easy or safe. This incarnational control narrative should shape the remembering of all Christians; the story we're in subverts, and is dangerous to, all other stories because it necessarily refutes secular notions of progress or ideological utopias and contradicts the idea that all past time is lost. And so the Christian historical imagination should be sacramental, and in a way that echoes the incarnational and sacramental memory of the Christian church when we celebrate the central sacrament of the church, the Eucharist, the Lord's Supper. The Eucharist is the sacrament in which we remember what the map depicts. History has meaning because it is a resurrection story; time has fullness because God loved us first. This should be a formative insight for how Christians do history. Surely there is hope that makes a difference, to believe that history, like all of creation, is an act of God's infinite and ceaseless love.

These are some of the lessons that a reading of a theologian like Metz can offer us. But what difference do they make? How do we model these in our practices? One of the purposes of the rest of this book is to explore the *extent* to which a field can be reimagined through the lens Metz gives us. Is the most we can hope for to nudge the discipline of history in a particular direction or to sharpen its focus? Or should we be looking to reimagine the story completely, retell it in a way which conflicts with the existing narratives? How can it be both recognizably and avowedly Christian and also recognizably historical at the same time? To borrow an analogy from the gospels for a moment, should we pour new wine into old wineskins? Or do we need new wineskins? As we go forward in this book, then, we will continue to raise the questions that Metz's vision of dangerous remembering asks of us as Christian historians. How shall we tell stories that honor the dead, the lost, the forgotten? When must we speak, and when must we remain silent? How must our remembering be ethical, relational, human? How should we re-form the practices and liturgies that shape our discipline?

34. Williams, *Why Study the Past?*, 96.
35. Eccl 3:15 (NIV).

CHAPTER 3

REIMAGINING OUR "HOW"
Re-Forming Our Practices

We observed earlier that a sense of shared practices was one—if not the—essential defining characteristic of history at present. These practices—centered on empiricism, the archive, fact-as-evidence, detachment—are how the bodies of knowledge that we call history are composed. But why do we do history this way? And can it be done differently? Should it be done differently? To ask what historians do is to probe the boundaries and rules of the historical profession. What or who do our practices serve? Who made the rules that we follow as practicing historians, and why? *How* does the past mean? All of our historical practices are in the service of something; none of us does history from a position of neutrality. These practices tell us much about who we are, about what we value and love as historians, and about how we think we can find meaning, understanding, or truth in the past.

Our re-forming has to go deep into our core practices if it is to meaningfully alter how we work. This means unpacking what we do, breaking it down, and trying to reveal what is going on. For instance, the work that historians do—why and how they do it and how quickly they do it—is underpinned by a series of choices we make as to how to work. These might be described in the following ways:

- What are we going to do research on and why?
- What materials we are going to need to read?
- How do we decide what needs to be read and what doesn't?

- How are we going to read them?
- How many things are we going to read?
- How much time do we have to complete them?
- How are we going to make sense of them?
- How are we going to present our findings?
- To whom is our work addressed?

The answers to these questions profoundly shape the practices that form the core of what the historian does when they do their work. So, how might we reimagine these practices? More particularly, how might we reimagine our practices as Christian historians? Reimagining our practices will start when we think about how we answer these questions, and then reflect upon how these answers will affect the way we work when we are in the archive, or reading documents, or taking notes, or writing a chapter in a book.

But let's take it back a stage further. Reimagining our practices will also require us to think about *what we bring* to our practices, the human virtues which shape what we do.

Reimagining Historical Practice Christianly: The Virtues of the Historian

What happens if we decide that an approach rooted in the modernist virtues—individualism, originality, scientific detachment, objectivity, knowledge production—should be abandoned? How might our practices change if our desire was to work in incarnational, collegial, loving, slow, and cooperative ways? If we bring a different set of values to our work, then maybe new (or old) practices or liturgies which embody these values will emerge. And maybe our work will look and feel different too.

Perhaps our emphasis should be on the following values:

- an incarnational model: walking lovingly and slowly alongside, not outside. Less detached, more involved, in which we stand with, not above, our subjects.
- a human approach: accentuating care, love, and compassion, rather than detachment and criticism.
- slowing down: paying full attention and being faithfully present.

- practices rooted in the communal, not the individual.
- solidarity: between researcher, the researched, and the audience. Historical research is about a community of scholars, authors, and readers in the present becoming connected not only with each other, but also across the centuries to those who went before us.

> If we asked these questions...
> *What if we sought wisdom, not originality?*
> *What if we sought advocacy rather than utility?*
> *What if we sought healing instead of explanation?*
> *What if we looked for hope?*
> *What if we asked how did this feel, not what does it mean?*
> *What if we sought delight and wonder, not understanding?*
> *What if we were seekers rather than finders?*
> ... then, what might our history look like?

This theological or sacred turn in the writing of history can provide a counterpoint to the values of modernity and its modernist impulses to classify, categorize, and analyze. In its stead, we root ourselves in the human and allow our spirits to be moved, energized, excited, and touched by the lives we read and write about. We think it might be worth outlining that this is not a rejection of modernist principles and practices *per se*—after all, much of what has been done has been insightful, stimulating, controversial, illuminating, useful and helpful—but rather a moving *beyond modernity*. This movement *beyond* entails different things. In some respects it will mean moving in a different direction. At other times it might look like an intensification of modernist practices. Perhaps it might mean repurposing our practices, deploying them for different ends. It will definitely mean doing things more slowly, more attentively. It will also mean rejecting some things too. It might mean looking back deep into the past. It might mean peering beyond the horizon.

We will, at some point, need to get some new wineskins for our new wine.

A Theological Turn in Historical Practice

Time for something more tangible. So how might we contrast the theological way of doing history with the values of modernity? The table set out below offers a quick comparison. This is, of course, a generalization, but it will serve our purposes here. On the left-hand side, we see some of the key values and ideals which underpin modernist approaches to studying the past. On the right-hand side, we have an alternative set of values and ideals which might form a different basis for our practices. We hope they do not need too much explanation.

Modernist	Theological
Detached	Incarnational
Skeptical	Loving
Absent	Present
Utility	Justice
Haste	Slow
Competition	Collegiality
Accumulation	Advocacy
Individual	Communal
Originality	Sharing
Personal Benefit	Common Good
The Archive	Memory, Voices, Images
Analysis	Narrative
Explanation	Healing
Reason	Empathy
Truth(s)	Truths

This is still rather abstract though. The purpose of this chapter is to propose new ways of doing history, new practices. How might this affect us when we open our books? When we visit an archive? When we begin to read a document or study a photograph? When we try and make sense of our research? When we start to write? We do not have all the answers, and we do not have the space to propose new ways of doing all the different aspects of what we do. Actually, we think this is something we need to do together anyway. We need to spend some time in earnest conversation about all this. But we will propose some ideas to kick-start this conversation.

So, we will pick three things. Firstly, how and why we read. Secondly, privileging the social context of our work. Thirdly, working with an ethic of service, humility, and other-mindedness.

Re-Forming History

1. Working Lovingly and Slowly: How Should We Read Our Texts?

Wisdom requires us to read everything carefully, with insight and nuance. But perhaps we need to think carefully about how we read, and why we read. The general skepticism about the possibility of objectivity and truth—and the overbearing dominance of irony, skepticism, cynicism, and pessimism that have accompanied it—have tended to create an ethic of suspicion toward what we read. Now this does not mean that we must naïvely accept truth claims or surface appearances. But it does perhaps suggest that we need to temper this with some other qualities and virtues. In particular, we should perhaps heed the instruction—as we embark on our research—to be "as shrewd as snakes and as innocent as doves."[1] This seems to combine the need for shrewdness, discernment, and practical wisdom, with a call for purity, integrity, and gentleness. Shrewdness evokes learning, listening, knowing when to speak, and when to stay silent. Innocence requires openness, an absence of malice, and a tender demeanor. This requires a delicate balance to be struck when reading a document: handling it carefully and wisely, but also tenderly and openly, willing to be surprised. Establishing some of the basic details of the source—dating, authorship/creator, audience, provenance—still seems a fruitful thing to do, so that a sense of the people involved can be known or at least begun to be known. Understanding their context, their influences, their motivations, their limitations and deficiencies will help us to appreciate the content and the significance of what we are handling. But perhaps it might not be the best place or way to start the process. A more interesting place to begin might be to examine oneself, and so to carefully consider how one is approaching your work.

What do we do when we read? Well, often the default settings for human readings of historical sources are to try and get what we need from this source, to find something that we are looking for, to become better informed, fill in a blank spot in our knowledge, or shed light on a puzzling or contentious episode or person. We want to perhaps be proven right in our opinion, or establish *the truth*. We often become a little suspicious of what we might find, too, rather unwilling to be too certain or trusting of what we see, read, or hear. Perhaps this distrust needs tempering with a different ethic of reading. A reading ethic which is marked by love, trust, and generosity of spirit should be our starting point. This is primarily because this reading should be seen as a sacred thing, not a suspicious thing. And that's

---

1. Matt 10:16 (NIV).

because our motivations for this reading should not be centered around what we can get out of it, or how we might use it, but instead we should be seeking delight in the act itself, recognizing the fundamentally human dimension of what we are doing. We should read as much for *formation* as for *information*.

There are probably two good starting points for our reading of historical texts, which should help us to see it more sacredly than suspiciously. The first is to think of oneself in regard to the other (whomever that may be) as being an uninvited reader into a private conversation, rather than someone who is uncovering a vast secret plot which needs to be exposed, as if somehow these things have been deliberately concealed. Being uninvited means thinking carefully about what you do with what you read, i.e., about your presence in the conversation. We are not necessarily unwanted. But we were definitely not in mind when the original conversation took place, and thus we should act accordingly. We should handle the material carefully, think about what we do with it, and consider the implications of our actions.

The second is to accentuate the human connections at play, and the essential qualities of familiarity, commonality, and community. The act of reading should perhaps be viewed as a reaching across the gaps—culture, belief, time, space, race, gender, language—which separate us from the people whom we are reading about. This notion of reading as a deeply communal act stands at odds with the rather solitary and individualized idea of reading which has dominated modernity. The widespread diffusion of literacy (clearly a good thing, by the way) put to death the collective reading and oral storytelling practices of other peoples at other times. Recovering a sense of reading as a shared human practice is, we believe, very important. The communal nature of our reading has two dimensions, and operates differently in each one. Spatially, the idea of shared reading connects us with the people around us: fellow practitioners, as well as those who read what we write and talk about. We read (and are read) to help others understand, to bring to light that which was hidden, but also so that others might read with us and help us to understand what is going on. We seek the wisdom of the group, and we share in the act with others who also delight in these things. But there is also a chronological dimension to this, too. We reach across time to read and we start to remember the people about whom we read. We consider, as a first thing, their humanity. We value their life and their dignity. And in this moment we start to connect the living and the dead. We bring them back to life and they sit and walk among us again. We, somehow, exhume and revive them.

So, before we start to read, we should consider our presence in the conversation. But *how* should we read?

Rather than clothing oneself in critical detachment at the outset, perhaps it is necessary (and more fruitful) to adopt a variety of different postures toward the material at hand, and read it multiple times in different ways in order to give it our fullest appreciation. Of all the different ways there are to read, three stand out. Perhaps the most important is to read with imaginative sympathy. We should look with sympathy at the human beings involved, and try to engage imaginatively with their viewpoints, concerns, fears, hopes, and ambitions. Second, we read not just to find things to use. Reading should be much more than finding things; it should be about a deep appreciation. We may find nothing of value to our work/project/book, but in trying to find something we may be missing a whole host of other things. Third, we should be reading slowly, immersively, deeply, plurally. The act of reading should retain its sacred character. It should not be viewed mechanistically (just decoding signs and symbols). It should not be approached functionally (just for what we can get out of it). It should not be rushed (so we can move on to the next task, or reach the end). It should not be done singularly (we should read many times and in many ways). No, reading should be a slow, profound, attentive, surprising act, rich in nuance, whereby we are savoring the words, seeking meaning, and acknowledging mystery and our limited understanding. It should connect with our minds, souls, reason, and our emotions, and in so doing it should connect us with our whole selves, and with others. As Eugene Peterson has observed, "reading is an immense gift, but only if the words are assimilated, taken into the soul—eaten, chewed, gnawed, received in unhurried delight . . . Reading that enters our souls as food enters our stomach, spreads through our blood and becomes . . . love and wisdom."[2]

The sustained attention and time that this type of sacred reading brings allows us to approach our texts in a number of ways, or to read them multiple times. We read it with imaginative sympathy. We read with empathy. We read with critical detachment. We read with curiosity. We move beyond the text, and we draw inferences, or we see behind the lines. In this way we come to experience the richness of what is on the paper, the

---

2. Peterson, *Eat This Book*, 25.

complexity and nuance involved, and it helps us to think new thoughts, give birth to new ideas, revisit old truths, and evaluate existing opinions.

So, in sum, our approach to reading should look something like this if we are to move beyond the functional, utilitarian approach of modernity:

- Self-examination: remember that *we are uninvited* and that there is a deeply human set of connections at play when we read;
- Reflect upon *why* and *how* we read before we begin to read;
- Then consider *what* we are reading.

Now this all probably sounds a little, well, idealistic, doesn't it? Imagine you are reading this (maybe skimming over it?) and thinking, "well, that's all well and good, but I have a deadline to meet, a paper to write, only an hour before my next class, or the kid wakes up, or I have to go to work . . . or . . . or." And that is the problem, right there. The cultural practices of modernity continue to produce modernist thinking and modernist outcomes. If we want to move beyond modernity in our historical practices we have to start approaching our texts in other ways. We have to develop new rhythms, habits, and practices which help us to resist the pressures of modernity and so begin the process of creating another world. It is, at root, an essentially spiritual act, rooted in tangible reading practices and requiring practice and commitment and time and care. The choice is ours.

2. A United Pursuit: Working with Others, Sharing with Others, Loving Others

The second reevaluation concerns the social context of our work, and especially the idea of history as a *united pursuit*. A discipline, to repeat Ludmilla Jordanova again, functions rather like a community of belief. It is a bounded community whose adherents share a set of beliefs and practices which distinguishes them from other groups. They share a deeply held commitment to the value of their discipline. They believe that the faithful and continued exercise of these practices will yield valid and reliable insights. They train others in these practices. They participate together in various contexts: places of learning, conferences, professional bodies, and the like. What unites historians is this shared understanding of the importance of a set of practices, and the value of using these in order to study the past.[3]

---

3. Jordanova, *History in Practice*, chaps. 1–4.

Re-Forming History

The discipline of history then seems to share some qualities with a community of belief. But the health of this community, its effectiveness, and its value, lie in how this community functions. If we are to move beyond modernity, then it is important that we accentuate and integrate the social, communal aspects of the discipline as far as possible, and temper the essential individualism of the (admittedly caricatured to some extent) lone heroic researcher which stands at the heart of modernity. This requires a consideration of some of the shared practices and conventions within which historians operate. One of the complicating factors of modernity was that in extolling the virtues of the individual scholar pursuing truth, these same scholars were then located in an institutional architecture which brought both competition and collegiality. So if we are to move beyond modernity, we must be looking to undercut the forces pushing us toward individualism and destructive competition and rivalry. This is not easy, given that the entire regime of training and preparation for the academic life is via the PhD (a notably singular and solitary life), and that the institutional setting for academic life exists within a nexus of resource scarcity and an abundance of labor (the reserve army of academics, or sessionals as we like to call them). But try we must.

Thus we need to recover the essentially social nature of what we do. This has to be seen as recovering something meaningful and valuable in its own right, not just for what it can do for each scholar to enhance his/her own output, or to prevent errors or problems from occurring (although these are obviously useful things too). The social context of learning should emphasize that scholarship should be done with others and for others. Our scholarly work demands that we allow others into our work at all stages: to consider ideas and hypotheses, to comment on proposals, to assist when there are problems, or to hold someone accountable for their views or conclusions. We should welcome others into our work. In this way we see our work as cumulative, cooperative, interdependent, and contingent. Others will come along later and improve or refute or confirm our work in the same way that we did with our ancestors. In this way we (once again) should be aware of the chronological and spatial dimensions of our work. We invite our contemporaries into our work as we research and write. We look back and take the best of what has been done before, and we write with our successors in mind. As the quote—made famous by Isaac Newton—says, "we see more and farther than our predecessors, not because we have keener vision or greater height, but because we are lifted up and borne aloft

Reimagining Our "How"

on their gigantic stature." This sense of connectedness—united across time and space—should be the bedrock of our scholarly work: united together in the pursuit of wisdom, knowledge, understanding, and truth.

This requires us to adjust our thinking. It requires us to recognize our debt of gratitude to those who have gone before, and also to write and research with care and responsibility. It requires us to exercise trust in others who will handle our work, and provide us with commentary and borrow or adapt or critique our ideas. It requires a posture of openhandedness and generosity: we study to share freely and openly what we find, not so that we can benefit or get ahead of the pack. Inviting others into our work is hard, and the potential is that others might take "our" work and use it for their own benefit. But this is the risk. Trust requires vulnerability. So there is work to be done in starting to function in a genuinely social and sociable fashion. Where might we begin?

We think a couple of things stand out, but these are just opening thoughts to a much bigger conversation that needs to be had within the profession (and not just within each discipline but as academics). Academics need to recover their sense of collective identity and responsibility to society as a whole and to each other, and resist those pressures which turn us against each other. This is no simple task, given the career and professional structures within which we operate. But as neoliberalism extends its reach into areas such as education and health care, so the corrosive effects of this on academic work and life need to be resisted. This can be done in myriad ways, but a grassroots shift in practices is as good a way as any to start. This means starting to work in ways which are deliberately collaborative and collegial. Write with others. Invite others into your work at an early stage, maybe using social media or blogging as a way to test new ideas, get feedback, and advance new lines of inquiry. Start a dialogue with others. This should help to combat those tendencies to do your work on your own in order to safeguard the originality of your approach or sources. It also opens you up to the thoughts and views of others. Collaborate and cooperate. The deeper structures of academic life also need to be addressed, but that is a much bigger, thornier issue than can be dealt with here. But it cannot and should not be ignored.

Finally, we need to rethink the pursuit of originality as the end of our work. This is not to say that original work is bad; that would be absurd. But the prize and prestige should not be reserved solely for the purveyor of originality. No, we should have an ethic of collaboration and sharing, prizing the discovery, not the discoverer. This critique of the pursuit of originality goes much deeper than the issue of the individualized mode of working. It also raises a broader question about the pursuit of knowledge and practicing knowledge as love, not power. The discipline has tended to privilege curiosity—the desire to know more and more, to try to know everything—as its default position. Yet this is in many ways, as Beth Barton Schweiger argues, knowledge as power and control. We pursue knowledge, and original knowledge in particular, not just for our own personal benefit, but because it gives us a sense of mastery, of control which we cannot get elsewhere. We aspire to know fully, universally, to acquire comprehension and understanding of our human past. And so we seek to possess knowledge about the past. But in doing so we flirt with this God complex. We can ignore people, control their lives as we tell their stories, or shape how they are perceived.[4]

Instead we need to pursue knowledge as love, not using the past and the people for our own needs, but to care for them. Knowledge as love should have only one aim. As Thomas Merton puts it, "Love seeks only one thing. The good of the one loved."[5] And pursuing knowledge as love should also remind us of our own limitations. We cannot know everything. We will never know fully. So perhaps our aspiration should be to love the limitations on us—for they remind us of our humanity, the contingency of our work, and our need of others—and to love the particular as well as the universal as we work to try and piece things together.

3. The Ethic of Historical Work: Humility, Service, Endlessness

There is a long list of personal and intellectual qualities required to practice history well. What needs rethinking are the spirit in which they are practiced and the motivations behind them, rather than the qualities themselves. Persistence, determination, attention to detail, honesty, integrity, transparency, empathy, and the like are all admirable qualities. A deeper issue lies in how and why we cultivate and demonstrate these qualities and habits of mind and action. Two things come to mind here: humility and service. We carry out our work with humility in order to serve those around us. This will manifest itself in myriad ways.

4. Schweiger, "Seeing Things."
5. Merton, *No Man is an Island*, 3.

Reimagining Our "How"

A crucial part of doing history (as with almost all intellectual life) is its endlessness. One of the destructive caricatures that has dominated academic life is the heroic scientist/scholar gloriously and tirelessly working away to establish the truth of what really happened. Now this is clearly a caricature, and most academics accept the contingency of what they are doing. But the myth of the elusive Holy Grail of research still lurks in the subconscious of most researchers, even if we rarely admit to it. We still hope that our work might just be the one that settles that question, or changes the field forever. This dragon needs to be slayed. We need to embrace the three impossibles of doing history. One, the impossibility of ever reading everything. Two, the impossibility of finding something that is not there. Three, the impossibility of ever writing the final word. This looks and sounds a lot like a kind of pessimistic postmodern defeatism. We can't know anything for sure, so let's give up and go home, or just do the best that we can, knowing that ultimately we will fail.

However, this need not be defeatism at all. In fact the recognition of these things should liberate us from a sense of defeatism and failure, of accepting contingency as a second-best state-of-being. Once we accept that we can never research everything (this powerful alluring idea that if we just do some more reading, visit one more archive, then we will have read everything there is to read and so we can start our work from this authoritative position of omniscience), that this idea of exhaustive research is a chimera, this frees us to approach our work differently. Moreover, if we embrace the idea that our own work is always only ever going to be a contribution to a story that will never end, that our work will have an incredibly short shelf-life, this too brings us into a different place. The humility of the scholar underpins this notion that we cannot do it all on our own, and that this thing we do is never-ending and that we can only ever know in part. We peer through a glass, darkly. We peer with others, and we peer for others. We peer for a short time. And so we start to delight in our limitations as humans and as scholars: temporariness, impermanence, endlessness. We can never know it all. Never understand it all. Never finish the story. Never read everything. The beauty of the historian's craft is precisely that it has no ending. If we inhabit this border between knowing and unknowing, and learn to look with humility upon our own best efforts (and those of others) we free ourselves from frustration and disappointment. What we don't know, or what still remains mysterious, becomes a task that hopefully someone else who comes after us will tackle.

Secondly, that when we work, we work for others, not ourselves. An ethic of service, one which is other-regarding, should be uppermost in our minds. A central part of this activity is to reconnect the work of the historians with the general public, rather than remaining cloistered. Historians, according to Justin Champion, "have an intellectual responsibility to make every effort to connect the past to the public: history is ultimately a cultural form of public property."[6] Additionally, our intellectual labors should create things that we seek to share, not possess, to delight in, not just use. Paul Griffiths prefers the idea of studiousness to curiosity. The imperative behind studiousness is studying to share freely what we have, whereas the imperative behind curiosity is to acquire sole possession of the knowledge.[7] And this is not just an act of service to our fellow practitioners (although that is part of it) and not just to our audiences either (students or readers or friends or hearers). It is also an act of service to those whose lives we read about. We work to give them a voice, make them present, bring them to life. Our work should be infused with this sense of responsibility to those who have gone before us. This is our act of service.

Thirdly, we work even though it seems mundane and ordinary. Much of our work is less than exciting, it has to be said. Hours and hours spent reading, sifting, noting, refining, rewriting, questioning, and revising. It is hard and often seemingly fruitless. Will anyone publish it? Will anyone read it? Will anyone like it? Does anyone care? This is where we have to be wary of the lure of the sensational, of the thrill of the pursuit. If we are driven purely by trying to find "that" document, or to reveal the "*New Interpretation!*" we will inevitably miss something. Our work requires a long, steady gaze at the lives we come across. If we hurry through our reading because it does not seem exciting or does not reveal what we hope to find, we are succumbing to the temptation of the superficial. If we learn to appreciate the minutiae, and the details, we start to see the world that has gone before us, and the people who lived before us, however unremarkable they might appear. When we learn to love the ordinary and the everyday in the people we encounter, maybe that causes us to see our own world and our own lives differently too.

And so we stop, we slow down, and we rethink our practices. We work from a hermeneutic of love and at a slow tempo, attentive to others and to ourselves. We work with others, for others, we acknowledge others, and we

---

6. Champion, "What are Historians for?," 169.

7. Griffiths, *Intellectual Appetite*, cited in Hauerwas, *Working with Words*, 136–37.

offer our work as service to all those around us, to all those who have gone before us, and all those who will come after us.

What shall we say then, by way of conclusion?

There is so much more that needs to be said and done when it comes to re-forming our core practices. This is merely the start of a long conversation we need to have. It starts with ourselves of course. But we need to do this together, not on our own. It takes courage to slow down. Work differently. We need each other to work this out.

Ironically enough, although this is a conclusion to this chapter, this is really just the starting point. The idea of re-forming history has caused us to look again at what we do, how we do it, and why we do it. In short, it has caused us to look at re-forming our liturgies. As we survey the practices of modernist history, we have come to appreciate the vast and diverse array of history that is out there now, and the diligence, passion, and sacrifices that lie behind it. We are also aware of the deficiencies of modernist history, and of the need to reorient our practices around the values of love, humility, solidarity, and collaboration.

If we pause for a moment, we will see that in fact we are not just thinking about what we do and how we do it. We are in fact thinking long and hard about why we do what we do, and for whom we do it. We will say more about this in due course. But at this point it is worth saying that what we are talking about is that historians must recover a sense of vocation and purpose for their work which goes way beyond the idea of studying the past for its own sake, or for the utility it brings historians in terms of their career, reputation, or remuneration. William Katerberg addresses this issue when he argues that our history must serve life, must serve the living and the dead.[8] The core attributes of the modernist project—accuracy and reliability—are merely the bare minimum requirements for the historian. They are a foundation: necessary, but not enough. The aim is to help build a different, better world.[9]

Katerberg notes Howard Zinn, who criticizes academic history and its ideal of studying the past for its own sake: "History that is written self-consciously to address a moral, social or political issue can indeed 'twist' the truth," he agrees. But nonconcern (the own sake ideal) can result in "another kind of distortion, in which the ore of history is beaten into neither a

---

8. Katerberg, "'Objectivity Question,'" 14–21.
9. Katerberg, "'Objectivity Question,'" 113.

ploughshare nor a sword, but is melted down and sold." Such pure history is, in effect, an economic commodity.[10]

If we start to reorient the purpose of our work around an ethic of service to others, then this places love at the heart of what we do, and in particular the biblical imperative to love the other, our neighbor, as we love ourselves. It replaces the concern for reliability, accuracy, and scientific detachment with the great challenge that faces our world: How do we love those others who are different from us?[11] And what role does history play in this? As historians, we have a responsibility to use our work and our talents to strive for a better world. As human beings and global citizens, our scholarship should work to remove barriers and end the divisions which exist in our world. We should be historians *sans frontieres* in an intellectual world without borders. The heart of what we wish to see, though, is that history recovers its moral imperative to be something that authentically serves life: the lives of those who have gone before us, the lives of those around us, and the lives of those yet to come.

If we stop for a moment we will see that we are in fact starting to ask slightly deeper questions: What are historians for? Why do we have historians and why are we historians? The implication of all that we have said above is that if history is to recover its sense of a broader calling to serve the living and the dead, then this requires historians to recover a prominent public role for themselves. For we cannot afford to merely speak to each other in some private conversation, or confine our work to things that no one reads, or work solely for our own professional benefit or standing. For who or what does that serve? As Justin Champion says, "a book unread is not only mute, but dead."[12] The responsibility of the historian is to connect their audiences—present and future—to the people of the past. The responsibility of the historian is to tell the past in such a way that it is possible to reach the great mass of people out there in engaging and entertaining ways. The responsibility of the historian is to bring the wisdom and weight of the past to bear upon the present state of things. The responsibility of the historian is to help us all "to live well and faithfully in the present," and to peer hopefully into the future.[13] The responsibility of the historian is to be attentive to their world and to love it.

---

10. Howard Zinn, as quoted in Katerberg, "'Objectivity Question,'" 112.
11. Katerberg, "'Objectivity Question,'" 121.
12. Champion, "What are Historians for?," 168.
13. Katerberg, "'Objectivity Question,'" 121.

CHAPTER 4

THE POWER OF STORIES, THE WONDER OF NARRATIVE

> My becoming a history teacher can be directly ascribed to the stories which my mother told me as a child when, like most children, I was afraid of the dark... So I shouldered my subject. So I began to look into history—not only the well-thumbed history of the wide world but also, indeed with particular zeal, the history of my Fenland Forebears. So I began to demand of history an Explanation. Only to uncover in this dedicated search more mysteries, more fantasticalities, more wonders and grounds for astonishment than I started with, only to conclude forty years later—notwithstanding a devotion to the usefulness, to the educative power of my chosen discipline—that history is a yarn. And can I deny that what I wanted all along was not some golden nugget that History would at last yield up, but History itself, the Grand Narrative, the filler of vacuums, the dispeller of fears of the dark?[1]

"But all the stories were once real."[2]

What might it look like if we re-formed the core practices of the discipline of history? In this chapter, we will explore two key interconnected parts of the practice of history. We have argued that Christian historians ought to look beyond modernity, to not be held captive by the liturgies of our

1. Swift, *Waterland*, 52–53.
2. Swift, *Waterland*, 257.

discipline, but to remember dangerously (as Metz advises us), and to practice love of our neighbors, whether dead or living. As a way to survey this territory and consider the possibilities, we might profitably *look back* and *look around*. Firstly, we will *look back* to consider whether the premodern practice of Christian history from earlier times still has anything to teach us. Has modernist history lost anything that we can fruitfully recover? Secondly, we need to *look around* at how others from other disciplines and professions tell stories. By looking at how the past can be told, we will emphasize the importance of story, creativity, and imagination in history. This is not just in the content of what we do, but also the medium of our telling. Let us start by looking back.

Recovering the Christian Ways of Understanding the Past

Here's a strange story. It comes from the works of Eusebius of Caesarea (c. 260–339 CE), a scholar and historian who has often been called the "Father of Church History," and it occurs at a decisive moment in the life of the Roman Emperor Constantine in 312 CE. Locked in conflict with a rival claimant to the imperial throne, Maxentius, Constantine and his forces were greatly outnumbered on the eve of what came to be called the Battle of the Milvian Bridge. "Being convinced," Eusebius tells us, "that he needed some more powerful aid than his military forces could provide him," Constantine appealed to God—the Christian God, not the pagan gods of his ancestors—for divine intervention. The answer to his prayer was astonishing:

> He (Constantine) said that about noon, when the day was already beginning to decline, he saw with his own eyes the trophy of a cross of light in the heavens, above the sun, and bearing the inscription, *Conquer By This*. At this sight he himself was struck by amazement, and his whole army also, which followed him on this expedition, and witnessed the miracle.[3]

---

3. Eusebius, *Life of Constantine the Great*, quoted in McGiffert, *Nicene and Post-Nicene Fathers*, 489, 490. For an account of the ways in which this famous story became legend, see Van Dam, *Remembering Constantine*.

FIGURE 5

Let us leave Constantine staring into the sky at Milvian Bridge for a moment and consider the quality of strangeness. History can be strange. Historians often remark that the past is a foreign country, by which they mean that the past is inhabited by people who think, live, and act in ways that are often very different from ourselves.[4] Theologian Rowan Williams remarks in his wonderful book *Why Study the Past?* that "Good history makes us think again about the definition of things we thought we understood pretty well, because it engages not just with what is familiar but with what is strange."[5] And this is a strange story that strains the limits of our credulity. How should we read it? Literally? Metaphorically? What kind of Christian imagination do we see here? Is this history? Or something else?

Followers of Christ in the early church thought differently about history than we do, as have Christians in every era, of course. That they did so, and that their historical imagination is strange to us, should not be surprising or troubling. What can we learn from engaging the writings of strange Christian historians? As Christian students of history, how can we place ourselves in these venerable traditions of historical imagination in ways that are not anachronistic and that do not engage those ways of knowing the past with the assumption that our way of knowing the past is superior,

---

4. The phrase "the past is a foreign country" comes from the novel by L. P. Hartley, *The Go-Betweens*.

5. Williams, *Why Study the Past?*, 1.

more accurate, and more reliable? This is an important principle for historians living and working today. Our ways of engaging with the past are not the same as those who lived in other times, and those who lived (and live) in other places and who believe different things about the world. Does our historical imagination have room for other ways of looking at the past?

Christians, History, and the Roman Empire

Let's return to Constantine staring into the heavens, as Eusebius describes it, and that mysterious glowing cross in the sky. What are we to make of this story? Reading from today's vantage point, our first impulse might be to be skeptical. In the twenty-first century, we are trained as historians to rely on empirical standards of proof to affirm whether or not something can be deemed a fact (a problematic term in itself). Hypothetically, we might trust this story as true if we could travel back in time and view the phenomena for ourselves, or if there were another authentic primary source external to Eusebius's history that bears witness to what he is claiming. And although Eusebius tells us that the whole army of Constantine witnessed the miracle we might be perplexed for another reason—that is, in our secular, rationalist, scientific age, many of us no longer give miracles any credence. So we might substitute a natural explanation for the supernatural or the miraculous—perhaps the cross was a trick of the sun's refraction, for example. Or maybe Eusebius is lying, and his account is a fiction constructed to legitimize and defend his political and theological agenda. Having said all these things, however, it is still true that many Christians across the globe today would read the story as literally miraculous. Who are we to say the age of miracles is past?

Still, while these interpretive questions are not irrelevant, our point here is not to insist that Eusebius's miracle is true or false—it is rather to take a glimpse at how a Christian from a radically different cultural context saw and understood history. So some context and interpretation is in order. Eusebius was writing at a pivotal moment in the history of the Christian church, which was moving from its position as a marginalized and persecuted sect to the dominant religious institution in the Roman Empire. In 313 CE, Eusebius became bishop of Caesarea, and he participated (controversially, it seems) in the Council of Nicaea, the first all-church meeting that under Constantine's sanction developed the first statement of Christian orthodoxy, the Nicene Creed. At the council, it appears that Eusebius met Constantine himself, and developed a great admiration for him and even styled himself as a friend and confidante of the newly converted emperor. And he wrote many books and orations, including his ten-volume *Ecclesiastical History*, a narrative account of the church from the time of Christ to Eusebius's own time.[6]

Why look at Eusebius? We can capture a glimpse of two themes pertinent to our discussion—first, his *methodology*, and second, his *philosophy of history*. Eusebius's history has been described as "highly original in conception" and one which "reads quite differently from any classical history."[7] Thus it is important to understand that Eusebius wrote in reference to existing scholarly conventions devised by the Greeks and the Romans on the one hand, and by the ancient Hebrews on the other. The Greek historians Herodotus (c. 484-425 BCE) and Thucydides (c. 460-395 BCE) are often described as enacting an intellectual revolution by establishing critical history as a rational discipline, an enterprise that entailed seeking out the truth from falsehood by employing methods that remain foundational for the historical profession: comparing and analyzing primary sources by checking accounts with the evidence of eyewitnesses. That didn't exclude the fantastical from historical writing; Herodotus famously tells of giant gold-digging ants in what is now India, and the works of classical historians are filled with miracles, portents, and other oddities. In fact, Eusebius's cross in the sky hardly seems exceptional in this respect. Still, Herodotus's famous account of the Persian Wars (*The Histories*) and Thucydides's *The Peloponnesian War* were intended to diagnose the causes and lessons of these pivotal conflicts, with the understanding that leaders could "master the arts of politics, statecraft, and warfare only from the study of history."[8] We might see this as an early version of the oft-cited cliché about history, that those who do not know the past are condemned to repeat it. Two other features shaped this new view of the purpose of history writing. First, both historians were relatively secular and humanistic in their interpretations of causation: history was a product of human action and volition and was not the product of divine ordering, even though the gods did figure in historical narratives. And second, both assumed that history was relatively *cyclical*, that even if events do not repeat themselves in particularities, they do

---

6. See the biographical sketch in Louth, "Introduction," ix–xiii.
7. Burrow, *History of Histories*, 190.
8. Gilderhus, *History and Historians*, 17.

so in patterns. That is why these writers saw a pedagogical and instructive imperative in knowing the past as a guide for future action.

The classical ideal of history can also be seen in Clio, the Muse of history. In classical mythology, the Nine Muses were the daughters of Zeus (the king of the gods) and Mnemosyne (the goddess of memory). They were the patron goddesses of poets and musicians, but over time this extended into other artistic areas, including comedy, tragedy rhetoric, harmony, and of course history. The Muses were said to have considerable powers to heal and comfort those who were sick or melancholy. Gifted by her mother with memory, Clio inspired others to creatively tell stories about the past in song, poetry, and narrative.

Clio would be called upon to assist the historians, to inspire them in their work, which was about celebrating the heroic deeds or acts of figures from the past. Peter Hoffer notes that the people who listened to the followers of Clio held them in high esteem for their ability to entertain and capture their imaginations.[9] The telling of the past in classical Greece required divine inspiration from Clio to assist the historian. And this inspiration took the form of stories and songs and poetry which instructed their listeners, but also entertained, enchanted, and inspired.[10] History was only in part about instruction. It was also about celebrating heroic deeds and developing creative skills—poetry, lyrics, music, story—to help their audiences feel the past and to fire their imaginations.

Another frame of reference that informs Eusebius's history writing is the Hebrew biblical tradition, which understandably was deeply influential on Christian thought. The differences between classical and biblical history are many, in that the latter is viewed as providentially guided and divinely inspired. God is the mover of history. And unlike the generally cyclical mode of classical history, biblical history is *linear*: there is a beginning (Creation) and an end (the Fall to an Apocalypse or Last Judgment). History is thus purposive and directional.[11] Suffice it to say, Eusebius draws more from the biblical tradition of history than the classical. In a profound sense, the history that Eusebius is seeing and writing is continuous with scriptural history, not distinct from it. In other words, Eusebius makes no arbitrary dividing line between biblical time and his own time, as we are prone to do; biblical history *is* contemporary history. The metanarrative

9. Hoffer, *Clio among the Muses*, 1.
10. Hoffer, *Clio among the Muses*, 1.
11. See Burrow, *History of Histories*, 179–85.

of Eusebius's church histories and martyrologies, like those of the Hebrew biblical narrative, is a story of God's redemption of history. But it is also the story of the church, and as such it is polemical and a work of partisan advocacy. He does not try to be neutral or objective. While the church had just emerged—almost miraculously—from a period of intense persecution, Eusebius still felt compelled to defend the church from its detractors.[12]

His methodology was also different in interest and content from its classical counterparts. Because church history was essentially so polemical, so attentive to discerning orthodox opinion from error and heterodoxy, Eusebius used his sources in a different way than his classical counterparts: *he selected his sources as witnesses to the truth as he saw it*. If on the whole the classical historians positioned themselves as neutral recorders of the facts (they weren't, but they often claimed to be) Eusebius was by no means a disinterested observer. He was a partisan of Christian orthodoxy and his narrative was constructed to prove the veracity and antiquity of Christian truth. His work is thus apologetic and fixed within the embattled tradition he was trying to defend. Small wonder, perhaps, that the cross in the sky was miraculous more than in a material sense; for Eusebius, it represented nothing less than the hinge of history, of God's astonishing intervention in history that was an unforeseen reversal of the church's fortune.

While not a historian, we can compare Eusebius's view of history with the philosophy of the early church's greatest theologian, St. Augustine of Hippo (354–430 CE). And in fact, most commentators on the evolution of Western and Christian historical consciousness see Augustine as much more influential, even much more foundational, than Eusebius. Most important, perhaps, is his sense of time, again derived from Hebrew or biblical conceptions of history rather than the general Greek idea of the cyclical and repetitive nature of the past. History instead has a clear linear direction, beginning with God's creation, moving to crisis with humanity's fall. And then the central events of human history—Christ's incarnation, death, and resurrection—would be consummated at the end of time when Christ's return marks the final victory of the city of God over the earthly city. Creation, fall, redemption—that is history's story, its meaning, direction, and purpose. The true story of history is the enactment of God's plan of salvation, in which humans are the object and not the subject of God's actions.

Our brief look at Eusebius will have to suffice as an example of Christian historical imagination before modernity. We might say, as a massively

---

12. Louth, "Introduction," xxxiv.

broad generalization, that almost all history written in the West before the Enlightenment was by definition *Christian* history, since Christian worldviews were so normative and universal.[13] It might be easy to dismiss these pre-Enlightenment Christian historians and theologians as possessing conceptual and imaginative language that simply no longer applies to how Christian students of history should understand the past today because our intellectual and imaginative context is so different. We can easily appreciate Eusebius and his works as products of a particular time and context, but it is more of a leap to see him as a theoretician of history whose views or practices are useful to us today. The stories they tell are too strange to take too seriously. Or are they? So what can we learn? Let's look briefly at four aspects of this massive body of literature and thought: in general, these authors had views of history that were *universal, providential, apocalyptic,* and *partisan*.[14]

By *universal*, we mean that these writers saw history, both sacred and profane, earthly and heavenly, as a single story. "All persons and all peoples are involved in the working out of God's purpose," R. G. Collingwood says, "and therefore the historical process is everywhere and always of the same kind, and every part of it is a part of the same whole."[15] Even if the subject of the history was local or national, it was still framed in the context of creation or salvation history. Today, we suggest, most historians do not see the past through the controlling narrative of universal history. There is no singular story being told really, no overarching narrative framework. An interesting new attempt, however, is the idea of "Big History," a conceptual framework for understanding the human past developed by David Christian. Let's quote him at length as he describes it:

> One of the things we asked ourselves, as we were trying to put together this story and trying to put together a coherent story that linked what we think of as the natural sciences and the humanities, was what sort of story would emerge at the end of this? In the past, say in the Christian tradition, or in fact, in all cultural traditions, you have unifying stories. We don't seem to have one in the

---

13. This is a problematic generalization, to be sure, made in the interests of time and space. Some might argue for the secular character of Renaissance historians like Machiavelli and Vico, for example.

14. Three of these four characteristics are how Collingwood describes Christian historiography; the fourth used by Collingwood is *periodized*. See Collingwood, *Idea of History*, 49–52.

15. Collingwood, *Idea of History*, 49.

> modern world. I'm talking about the natural sciences here. Many scientists are so worried that a concern for meaning, or story, or significance, or purpose will somehow warp the mapping process that scientists are engaged in. At the methodological level, that's true. You don't let your preconceptions warp what you're doing. But at an ontological level, I don't think that is true. In modern science, and I include the humanities here, science in a German sense of science—rigorous scholarship across all domains—in modern science we've gotten used to the idea that science doesn't offer meaning in the way that institutional religions did in the past. I'm increasingly thinking that this idea that modernity puts us in a world without meaning—philosophers have banged on about this for a century-and-a-half—may be completely wrong. We may be living in an intellectual building site, where a new story is being constructed. It's vastly more powerful than the previous stories because it's the first one that is global. It's not anchored in a particular culture or a particular society. This is an origin story that works for humans in Beijing as well as in Buenos Aires. It's a global origin story, and it sums over vastly more information than any early origin story. This is very, very powerful stuff. It's full of meaning. We're now at the point where, across so many domains, the amount of information, of good, rigorous ideas, is so rich that we can tease out that story. [16]

The prevalence of pluralism and specialization and the ubiquity of the nation-state as the basic building block of the modern world has seemingly undercut the idea of a universal story. But maybe there are signs that this is changing. And maybe this offers a way for Christian historians to think about a new universal history.

Next, premodern historians understood and practiced history through a *providential* lens. Today we have a shallow understanding of the notion of providence, however. We associate a providential view of history with the notion that God directs all of human events, that God is the agent of causation in history and that God is somehow directly controlling all things like pieces on a chessboard. Implicit in providentialist readings of history, too, is the idea that God takes sides in human events, that he intervenes—miraculously at times—to spare his people or smite his enemies. God controls all events; everything is in God's hands and reflects his will. Many unmodern historians, of course, saw such providential events through the lens of chauvinistic self-interest. A famous example is how the British interpreted

---

16. Christian, "We Need a Modern Origin Story," paras. 12–14.

their defeat of the Spanish Armada in 1588. The Catholic monarch of Spain, Philip II, plotted a massive invasion of Protestant England with a view to return it to the one true faith. The English faced astounding odds in ships and manpower, but the massive Spanish fleet was destroyed by a storm and the English were spared. The English viewed this as a miraculous intervention by God on behalf of the Protestant and English cause: "He blew his winds, and they were scattered."

There is a richer dimension to unmodern providentialism, however. Theologian Scott Bader-Saye has proposed that we no longer take providential readings of history seriously because we are used to naturalistic explanations for events and because natural catastrophes seem problematic to attribute to a benevolent God. "Providence," Bader-Saye argues, "has to do with the conviction that our lives and our world constitute a coherent story, a drama, in which God and humankind, together, drive the story toward its proper conclusion." This loss of a rich understanding of providence in our historical imagination is unfortunate because it is essentially a hopeful framework: "Providence is the conviction that through it all God's story cannot be lost, and thus God's hopes for the human story cannot be thwarted."[17] And we ought to think of providence as a narration, a type of storytelling, reading our stories and histories in a figurative way in which we find patterns that reveal truths about God and the world.[18] Figurative (not literal or scientific) interpretations of providence also allow us to see meaning in the rupture of suffering without sanitizing it in platitudes or passivity—a meaning mirrored paradigmatically in the story of Christ's death and resurrection—and allows us to be willing "to find our story in God's story and in so doing to have hope that tragedy is not the end."[19] Certainly that does not remove the abiding uncertainty or mystery of the meanings of events and patterns in history, yet we can have trust in knowing what story we're in even if its full meaning is outside our knowledge and understanding. There is faith and trust here, of course, but not passivity, since we are called to participate in the story God has given the world. This understanding of providence as a kind of narrative imagination is perhaps closer to how unmodern historians understood the past. Even when other aspects of their histories seem bizarre and strange to us—the miracles, the ease with which they saw portents as signifying God's favor or sanction,

---

17. Bader-Saye, *Following Jesus*, 79.
18. Bader-Saye, *Following Jesus*, 80.
19. Bader-Saye, *Following Jesus*, 85.

and the like (but wait, maybe we still do that!)—this deeper sense of providence as the referent for understanding history is not natural for us.

Nor is a third aspect of unmodern historical imagination—the *apocalyptic*. We are accustomed to think of the Apocalypse, when we do, as the cataclysmic event by which God ends history at the end of human time. The Apocalypse is the end of the story, as it were. Most simply stated, Apocalypse "is shorthand for Jesus Christ." It is the sense that "what occurs in the history of Jesus Christ is unsurpassed and unsurpassable"; there is no reality that transcends the revelation of Jesus Christ.[20] Apocalyptic history is history "which leaves no reserve of space or time or concept or aspect of creation outside of or beyond or undetermined by the critical, decisive, and final action of God in Jesus Christ."[21] Thus the revelation of Christ in history is dangerous to alternative conceptions of time and history. In the premodern period, this sense of Apocalypse as shocking revelation *in history*, not just at the end or outside history, was very prevalent. God is always showing himself, God is always doing. There is a secret divine design in the shape of human history, which lies beyond our ability to perceive it until we encounter the revelation of Christ in history. Then the design is unveiled.

Finally, Christian history was *partisan*. It took sides. It identified itself with a particular cause. It presented itself as part of the longer tradition of the history of God and his dealings with his people, and also was used to advocate for the interests of the Christian church, to defend it, legitimate it, protect it. These historians inhabited the story they were telling, and bore witness to the world as they saw it from their standpoint, and also as part of a world that was also hovering into view. It was an explicitly situated history. These historians were deeply engaged when they wrote their work. This has also found an increasing resonance across the twentieth century amongst all types of historians. The acceptance of the impossibility of objectivity has been accompanied by an acceptance of the desirability of the explicitly situated historian. There are many examples, but one will suffice here. George Mosse, a historian who had to flee from totalitarianism at a young age, became convinced that the historian should not pursue detachment, but engagement. History should be infused with an ethical imperative. He went on to say that, "It took me many years to realize that writing about historical problems which have affected one's own life was no barrier

---

20. Harink, *Paul among the Postliberals*, 68–69.

21. Quoting Harink, *Paul among the Postliberals*, 69, with respect to defining apocalyptic theology.

which stood in the way of understanding historical reality."[22] Mosse was an advocate for passionate commitment on the part of the historian, something the early Christian historians also held as inherent to the work of the historian. History was supposed to be passionate and partisan.

History that is universal, providential, apocalyptic, and partisan. How might these ideas shape how we view the past? How we study the past? How we think about the past? And how we tell the past? And so now we're back at Milvian Bridge with Constantine, looking at that cross in the sky, shocked and amazed. Should we dismiss it as naïve? Or suspicious? Or can we open our imagination and think creatively and carefully about this sense of the past?

Looking Around: How Can We Tell the Past?

On to our second question. *How can we tell the past well?* What is the best way to tell others about the past? This is a question that until recently had received surprisingly little attention amongst historians and others. Instead, historians have waged wars over truth and falsehood, fact and fiction, objectivity and subjectivity, theory and empiricism. Thankfully, this omission is starting to be addressed. There is now increased activity amongst historians and others in exploring the ways in which the past can be told, and in evaluating the relative merits and problems of different ways of telling, including literature, film, and television, as well as through the more traditional modes of academic writing. Barbara Tuchman notes that the historian is (or should be) an artist.[23] As we unpack this topic we will come across an inescapable tension, as described by John Tosh, who in reflecting upon the lack of clarity around historical writing notes that, "In the main this is because of the different and sometimes contradictory purposes behind historical writing, and above all of the tension which lies at the heart of all historical enquiry between the desire to re-create the past and the urge to interpret it."[24]

Tosh notes the dominance of three types of historical telling: description, narrative, and analysis (although these divisions are not so clear-cut in practice, as most historians blend all three in their work).[25] We will

22. Mosse, *On the Occasion*, xxviii–xxix.
23. Tuchman, *Practicing History*, 25–64.
24. Tosh, *Pursuit of History*, 147.
25. Tosh, *Pursuit of History*, 147.

briefly evaluate some of the approaches to telling the past, and think carefully about how we might tell the past in ways that are authentic, engaging, creative, and truthful. Can professional historians learn anything from the feature film, the TV documentary, the novel, the magazine? Can we do it better? Differently?

The telling of the past has evolved quite dramatically over the centuries. For most of the time that humans have recorded and written about the events of the past, the idea of story has been paramount. The Greek term *historia* conveys the idea of inquiry or investigation, and also a narrative, a record of events, a story. Indeed this divide between the idea of history as poetry or story, and history as inquiry, investigation, or analysis has never been resolved. Classical history conveyed the idea of history as a story designed to inspire, but also produced the works of Thucydides and Herodotus as outlined above. Medieval chroniclers sought to provide a particular type of story, filtered through their religious worldview. The long march toward history as a rational-scientific type of knowledge—written in a predominantly analytical mode or style—began during the Enlightenment, but accelerated in the late nineteenth and twentieth centuries. In particular, the twentieth century saw a gradual shift toward analytical, problem-oriented history writing. But the appeal of narrative as a form of telling the past never waned. What this has resulted in is history being told as different types of narrative, essentially. Before we delve into the variety of ways the past can be told, we should perhaps ask: Why do we feel the need to tell the past as narrative?

This is a very large topic, but four things seem to stand out. Firstly, the narrative—as a "dynamic unfolding of sequences of human actions"—is probably the most effective representation of the way that humans perceive time and live and act in the world.[26] Humans seem to be "story-perceiving beings."[27] Narrative thus seems to not only represent how people understand themselves and their own world, but also connects people to the past: as they read history as narrative, it seems to cohere and make sense. It communicates the passage of time, something essential to our knowledge and understanding of the past. Secondly, narrative works as a form of telling the past. It brings coherence and sense to a complex field. It is able to do justice to the issues of contingency and possibility and accident. It is able to account for the role of human agency in the historical process (either

---

26. Roberts, *History and Narrative Reader*, 5.
27. Lemon, "Structure of Narrative," 124.

individually or collectively). It is in many ways a pragmatic decision: it is the best means of telling the story of the past that seems to emerge from the research of the historian. Thirdly, narrative is also adaptable and flexible. It can be combined with description and/or analysis. It can be done at different levels (micronarratives or grand macronarratives). It can be done at the level of the individual or the collective. It can convey both what it felt like, as well as the more impersonal elements of the past (context, circumstances, and the like). And fourthly, as a literary exercise, narrative can be entertaining and engaging. It can use suspense, surprise, irony, humor, pathos, and imagination to connect people to the past.[28]

Narrative has its weaknesses, of course, which was in part the reason why there began to be a shift toward an emphasis upon analysis and problem-solving in the telling of the past. In particular, narrative does not do a very good job on the whole of historical explanation, notably when dealing with complex questions of causation. Narrative can communicate the twists and turns and surprises of the outbreak of World War I for example, but cannot really explain how the different factors are connected, which factors were most important, and why. That type of assessment requires a more analytical approach, which weighs different factors against one another. Narrative is not just an innocent story either. It contains within itself an interpretative framework. The material must be sifted and selected. The start point and end point must be selected. The story has to be told from a particular standpoint, and with the benefit of hindsight. Narrative tends to favor the short-term focus and the individual, over the long-term and the impersonal factors in historical explanation. They tend, by their very practice, to simplify complex events, and to bring coherence to chaos, and completeness to what is eternally unfinished. And at a deeper level, the narrative is clearly not the past, but merely a story told about the past, which makes it hard to assess how accurate it might be, given that the thing it is referring to—the past itself—is gone and is irrecoverable.[29]

These weaknesses of narrative are the reasons why historical telling has evolved over the years. Theory has been used by historians of different persuasions instead of narrative, especially those like Marxist or *Annaliste* historians, who have a bigger picture that they wish to explore or verify.

---

28. See Tosh, *Pursuit of History*, chap. 6, and Roberts, *History and Narrative Reader*, for extended discussions of narrative forms and their value to the historian. See also Munslow, *New History*, chaps. 7 and 8.

29. Tosh, *Pursuit of History*, chap. 6.

Thematic approaches use the idea of solving a problem as the central part of their approach. The main form of historical telling, though, in print form, is the analytical narrative, which seeks to combine elements of problem-solving, analysis, explanation, and evaluation with a loose narrative-type approach. Narrative has also evolved in other ways. Some have gone very small (micronarratives) or very large (master or grand narratives). Some have reversed the flow of time, narrating events in reverse. Some have opted to narrate from multiple points of view, to increase the plurality of possibilities in the past. We will come back to this point in a moment. First we need to examine the forms that telling the past can take.

Most of the telling about the past is done through writing: a book, an academic journal article or a magazine, a blog post. The audiences for these are quite (in some cases very) limited. Increasingly though, the mass consumption of history in the public sphere is done in the following ways:

- Feature films
- TV documentaries
- Video games
- Social media
- Museums and heritage sites
- Historical novels

The fact that these forms of history are designed for mass consumption by the public (rather than for the more restricted audience of peers and/or students) suggests that this is something quite different from academic history, in two ways. One, there is a commercial imperative behind much of this. It is designed to sell or attract viewers or visitors or followers. Second, it is designed with a much bigger, more disparate audience in mind, and so it has to have broad appeal both in terms of the different groups it appeals to, but also it must appeal to more than just human intellect and reason. It has to combine this with a deeper appreciation of emotion, passion, identity, and empathy.[30]

But do these different forms change the way people experience the past? What can academic historians learn from this, if anything? There are three things that this rendering of the past provides, which are either absent or only weakly present in academic texts: an emotional, immersive

30. Hunt, "Reality, Identity and Empathy," 843–58.

experience of the past; the possibility of reenactment; and authorial control. At the center, though, is the role of the human imagination, and the search for *understanding* (what was it like to live then?) rather than *explanation*.[31] Let us take these one at a time.

Immersion and Emotion and Experience

The demands of commerce and audience engagement mean that the non-textual forms of history are searching for ways to allow the viewer/participant to identify with the story, game, or exhibit. This means providing an immersive emotional engagement, giving them a sense of the lived experience of the past. Cinema, TV, and heritage sites try to create this sensual experience of the past where you can see, hear, touch, and smell the past all around you. The visual experience allows for a sense of recreating the past: the dress sense, the architecture, the manners, and the customs are all brought to life before our eyes. The kinetic experience of film—the ability to show the unfolding of time and change across time—is also another dimension which is often absent in textual representations of the past. The use of story in cinema also humanizes and personalizes the past: it compels us to identify with the key characters and their joys, desires, hopes, and failings.[32] We can see this even more clearly with heritage or living history sites, which employ actors to interact with visitors, staying in character the whole time.

Reenactment

The experiential aspect of telling the past is also reflected in this idea of reenactment. This can be described as, "the act of imaginative re-creation that allows the spectator to imagine that they are witnessing again the events of the past."[33] Reenactment thus calls for a double exercise in imagination: the imagination of the creator, and the imagination of the viewer/game player/visitor. The imagination is deployed to create a sense of reality or verisimilitude, which seeks to allow the sense of "witnessing again," as if

---

31. Hunt, "Reality, Identity and Empathy," 843–48.

32. See the extensive body of work of Robert Rosenstone, most notably *History on Film/Film on History*. See also Engelen, "Back to the Future," 555–63.

33. Burgoyne, "Balcony of History," 552.

the person has been physically transported to the event in the past and is on hand to see "what happened."[34] This idea of bringing a vanished world to life, and then inviting people in so they can experience it, is an extremely powerful one, and accounts for the great appeal of reenactment as a way of telling the past to a mass, diverse audience.

Authorial Control and Counterfactuality

Video games offer one unique element in the telling of the past: as the player is in control of the character within the game (or the direction of the game), they are able to alter the flow of history, as it were, by making different choices, or taking different decisions within the historical context. This enables an exploration of counterfactuality to be played out, which is driven by the player themselves (albeit within a range of options programmed by the designers and producers of the game). In every other medium, the author or designer has control over the narrative. In the example of video games, control is shared between the designer and the player, allowing for far greater interaction. The ability to alter the past also provides for intriguing possibilities in reimagining the past along the lines of "what if?"

The rise of historically based console games has coincided with an explosion of interest in exploring counterfactual scenarios in print.[35] A whole swathe of books and articles have appeared (usually dealing with questions around war, politics, and diplomacy) which have really turned counterfactualism into a cultural phenomenon in its own right. The question "what if?" has now become almost as commonplace as "what?" or "why?" or "when?" or "who?" This is not the time to go into the reasons for the ubiquity of counterfactualism at present. More interesting, perhaps, are the claims that counterfactualism makes about accidents, contingency, choice, and alternative scenarios. This shift toward an exploration of what might have happened—and not what did happen and why—has been criticized for being a form of wishful thinking, of "if-onlys" rather than "what-ifs." But the use of historical imagination, alternative futures, and different pasts contained within counterfactualism make it an intriguing form of history.

---

34. Burgoyne, "Balcony of History," 552.
35. See, for example, Ferguson, *Virtual History*; Evans, *Altered Pasts*.

Re-Forming History

History, Truth, and Fiction? Or Truth or Fiction?

Before we conclude this section, it is worthwhile to highlight one important question: Is there a place for intentionally fictional elements in the telling of the past? This is a difficult question, of course. The use of fiction clearly on one level undermines the truth claims of history. If a particular telling of history blends fictional and nonfictional elements, how do we know which is which? If history can be told purely as a work of the imagination, then any rendering of the past is possible, which can lead to the denial of the historicity of certain events. It is also, it can be argued, a denial of the moral responsibility of the historian, to tell the truth on behalf of the dead, particularly those who have no voice, and require that their story be told.[36] But perhaps we need to narrow the gap between history on the one hand and fiction on the other. Firstly, there is an inherently literary quality to the writing of history which means that it has much in common with poetry and the writing of novels. The story must be imagined, plotted, planned. Events must be fused into a coherent narrative, and the connections between them described. It is an inherently creative act. Secondly, fiction tells us truths even though it may not be true. A compelling expression of this idea comes from novelist Tim O'Brien. In his book *The Things They Carried*, a novel about the Vietnam War from an American perspective, O'Brien posits two kinds of truth: story-truth and happening-truth. In an extended passage, O'Brien notes that,

> It's time to be blunt. I'm forty-three years old, true, and I'm a writer now, and a long time ago I walked through Quang Ngai Province as a foot soldier.
>
> Almost everything else is invented.
>
> But it's not a game. It's a form. Right here, now, as I invent myself, I'm thinking of all I want to tell you about why this book is written as it is. For instance, I want to tell you this: twenty years ago I watched a man die on a trail near the village of My Khe. I did not kill him. But I was present, you see, and my presence was guilt enough. I remember his face, which was not a pretty face, because his jaw was in his throat, and I remember feeling the burden of responsibility and grief. I blamed myself. And rightly so, because I was present.

---

36. Some interesting pieces which examine this relationship are: Steedman, *Dust*; Longxi, "History and Fictionality," 387–402; Cohen, "An Essay in the Aid," 317–32; Schama, *Dead Certainties*; White, "Historiography and Historiophoty," 1193–99; Pouncy, "History, Real and Invented," 343–52; Hart, "Between History and Poetry," 568–88.

> But listen. Even that story is made up.
>
> I want you to feel what I felt. I want you to know why story-truth is truer sometimes than happening-truth.
>
> Here is the happening-truth. I was once a soldier. There were many bodies, real bodies with real faces, but I was young then and I was afraid to look. And now, twenty years later, I'm left with faceless responsibility and faceless grief.
>
> Here is the story-truth. He was a slim, dead, almost dainty young man of about twenty. He lay in the center of a red clay trail near the village of My Khe. His jaw was in his throat. His one eye was shut, the other eye was a star-shaped hole. I killed him.
>
> What stories can do I guess, is make things present.
>
> I can look at things I never looked at. I can attach faces to grief and love and pity and God. I can be brave. I can make myself feel again.[37]

Both history and fiction can convey truths about the past, and perhaps in some cases the fictional work can be a more powerful conveyor of truths. The relationship between history and fiction is further complicated by the genre of historical fiction: an entirely fictional account but set within the past. Fiction, according to Carolyn Pouncy, is the exploration of how the human mind solves problems. It is primarily about the internal mental world of the key protagonists. When this is set within a historical context, it can be a highly illuminating genre. She argues that well-written historical fiction not only can reveal the past to some extent, but also it can show how the concerns of the past differ from those of the present. More historians should write historical fiction, she notes, because they have become accustomed to trying to recreate the assumptions and values of people who lived in different times, different places, and different ways. They can (hopefully) do it well.[38] Historical fiction has an important place in the spectrum of telling the past, she concludes:

> Recreating the emotions of the past, establishing interest among potential students, exploring paths not taken, communicating outside the realm of academic history, raising questions that only research can answer and answering questions that research cannot: these tasks belong to the realm of historical fiction.[39]

---

37. O'Brien, *Things They Carried*, 171–72.
38. See Pouncy, "History, Real and Invented."
39. Pouncy, "History, Real and Invented," 352.

Re-Forming History

Robert Rosenstone says much the same about the historical fiction film, which shows us the past in new ways and reaches a huge audience. John Demos argues that there are two elements of writing historical fiction that novelists can show to historians. The first is what he calls "scrupulously close attention to significant human details."[40] Researching the minutiae and the mundane aspects of human life are crucial to the novelist, and the same imperative should be present for the historian. Demos calls this a concern for the textural quality of the past: what it feels like, the threads, weaves, creases, and the like. This should be just as much a concern as the structural qualities of the human past.[41] Secondly, Demos goes to the other extreme, from the minutiae to the biggest questions of all, and calls for historians to lose their fear of thinking and talking about human nature and the human condition on a grand scale, "We do not as historians usually claim human nature as part of our professional territory. Should we continue to leave the most basic, universal and personally significant parts of all of our lives to novelists, poets, philosophers, religious leaders and their like? I hope not."[42]

We hope not, too.

So, there is clearly a place for historical fiction in the telling of the past, and much that historians can learn from novelists and filmmakers, novels and films, in how we tell the past and what we say when we try and tell it. As Margaret Atwood says, "no-one can tell all the stories there are."[43]

Clearly there are similarities between history and fiction. History and the novel and poetry are on some levels comparable. But this does not mean that they are identical, of course. The story put together by the historian is not entirely a work of the imagination, but is structured and bound by the work done with sources. Thus, it combines in itself both the literary and poetic elements, and also an infrastructure of evidence, corroborated facts, and the like. Carolyn Steedman also highlights an essential difference between the novelist and the historian. The novelist has been there all along. The novel is the work of their imagination. The characters are brought to life and given color and texture by the author. The end is already known. In history by contrast, there is no end. No one knows how the story will

---

40. Demos, "In Search of Reasons," 1528.
41. Demos, "In Search of Reasons," 1529.
42. Demos, "In Search of Reasons," 1529.
43. Atwood, "In Search of Alias Grace," 1516.

end because it is endless.[44] This is the limitation that history places on the human imagination. *We don't know the end of the story.* The other contrast between the historian and the purveyor of fiction, as Sol Cohen notes, is the distinction between someone who creates characters, and someone who works with people who once were (or still may be) alive. We have to be very aware as historians that we have the power to turn real people into characters in a story: "who creates the story: the individual who lived it or the historian who writes it?"[45]

Let us conclude this chapter by considering how we might reimagine the telling of the past in light of the above. We observed the tension between the desire to recreate the past and the urge to interpret it. We have noted the problem of the "poetic" approach versus the "rational-scientific" approach to telling the past. We have seen that the past that is told in the public sphere emphasizes feeling, emotion, experience, empathy, and identity, whereas academic history has tended to prefer the rational, the analytical, the explanatory, history as problem-solving.

Perhaps the way forward is not to see this as an either/or. Perhaps the way forward is to see this as a creative tension, a both/and issue. Indeed the mutual tempering that poetry brings to reason and that humane feeling brings to analysis is in fact vital. Rationalists and Romantics need each other. And perhaps history has a part to play in bringing them together and seeing what emerges. One of the puzzles around the telling of the past is the way that historians over the last hundred years or so (with some notable exceptions) have tended to detach themselves from the public sphere and retreat into the deserted corridors of academia. Public, popular, storied history has thus on the whole been left to others to do (sometimes with the assistance of professional historians). This retreat has created this opposition between public and academic history, between poetry and analysis, between experience and explanation. Maybe now it is time to end this opposition.

We believe that historians must take up their role in the public sphere again. We must write good history, of course, but we should also tell our stories in other ways. We must devote more of our energy and thought to the question of how we tell the past, what form we will use, and which audience we wish to reach. We should consider the telling as a craft which needs to be honed. We should experiment with the new technology that is

---

44. Steedman, *Dust,* 147.
45. Cohen, "An Essay in the Aid," 328.

available. We should collaborate with videographers, photographers, artists, and animators. We should use elements of fiction, but we should be clear about when we are using them. We need to dive down to the minutiae of human life and wrestle with the deepest questions of human existence. Historians have the greatest repository of human stories at their fingertips. It is time to break free of the self-imposed constraints of academia and use our historical imagination to tell the past in new and old ways. Matthew Lyons poses a challenge to all professional historians and students of history:

> ... do historians challenge themselves enough to find an appropriate form for their ideas? They strive for originality of research and analysis, but how often do they strive for originality or inventiveness of form? The book or the long-form essay may still be the best format historians have for sustained and rigorous argument. But do they default to it out of admiration, laziness or cultural deference? After all, today's cultural and technological fragmentation and diversity offers enormous opportunities for generically—and therefore intellectually satisfying—creativity to those with the requisite talent, ambition and desire.[46]

We need to tell the past differently. We need to reach new audiences. We need to become reacquainted with the public dimension and significance of our work. Let's work together to see what that looks like. Let's harness our talent, collaborate, and see what turns up. We need to tell our stories differently, and also perhaps tell different stories, stories which promote hope, healing, and justice. We need to recover our public voice, and we need to learn to live with and work within the creative tension between poetry and analysis, imagination and intellect, understanding and explanation, reason and emotion.

---

46. Lyons, "Between Fact and Fiction," 46.

CHAPTER 5

DEATH OF A GUARDSMAN
Hesed *and the Historian's Calling*

"Every book I write starts with trip to the cemetery. I begin by listening to the dead, & aspire to end the apartheid between the living and dead."[1]

FIGURE 6

Let us begin with some foundational questions. But these questions are not—as one might think—questions such as: "What is history?" or "Can

---

1. Leonard Sweet (@lensweet), a tweet from 9:40 a.m., October 5, 2016 (https://twitter.com/lensweet/status/783693377527287809).

we ever tell the truth about the past?" No, we wish to throw the focus onto the historian—professor, history student, interested reader—instead and ask two questions.

Why?

Why do we—that is, professional historians—study the past? Why do we do it? Why do we teach, read, research, and write about the past? The question of what motivates those of us who engage in studying the past is seldom asked or answered. What are the mixture of different motivations and interests that underpin our work? Obviously there is the basic professional/material issue: it is a job. It pays the bills. In most parts of the Western world it provides a very good financial package. (Once you have tenure that is. The existence of the sessional/part-time scholar is exceptionally grim). But that is rarely the whole answer. There are always other things. Maybe it is something you love: the intrinsic curiosity/interest there is in studying human beings living in other times. Maybe it is a political or ideological motivation: you have a strong set of beliefs about the world, and you long to study them or use the past to tell others about them. Maybe it is the chance to write and be published. Maybe it is the chance to teach and help shape the thinking of others. Maybe it is a philosophical quest for the truth, or a desire to set the record straight. Maybe it is to right a wrong and pursue justice. Maybe it is to bring something to light that has never been explored. Maybe it is to try and understand the present more fully. Maybe there was nothing else you were any damn good at.

Often we read in general terms about why we should study the past, but rarely do we find a sustained engagement with the question of what motivates historians to keep doing what they do. Some historians have reflected upon the idea of history as a vocation or a calling, that there is some higher purpose behind what we do, beyond that of it being salaried work.[2] This can be related in part (in the post-secondary sector at least) to the position of professor. The professorial position arose as an expert in a field who declares publicly what they know and what they believe, and

---

2. The idea of the historian being "called," or thinking of themselves as having a vocation, is not a new idea of course. For some recent treatments of this idea, take a look at the following: Fea et al., *Confessing History*; Link, "Historian's Vocation," 373–89; Wells, "Beyond 'Religious History,'" 41–48; Kennedy, "Introduction," 1–6; Sweeney, "On the Vocation of Historians," 1–13.

who instructs others. Many see the professorial position as a calling. There are also those who see a more specific calling to write and teach about the past. In this way, the study of history helps others—readers, students—to understand their own world better, to be inspired to act, to remember what it means to be human. Studying history is also claimed to be a vehicle for personal transformation and development, almost akin to a spiritual discipline to help us grow, to become more empathetic and hospitable to others, to develop humility in the face of complex problems, and to locate our own situation in a much longer, deeper story.

For Whom?

The "why do I do this?" question is always a good one to ask of oneself in any walk of life. It is so easy to do what you have always done, but asking this question can lead us down some interesting paths and make us ask further questions. Deeper questions. Troubling questions. So, for example, what if we began by asking: What are our responsibilities to the people of the past? *For whom do we do what we do?* Who are our audiences when we write? When we sit for hour after hour in cold, dusty archives, for whom are we doing such diligent work? We have already outlined above that we have audiences in our classrooms (if we teach) and in the wider society (if we write). And of course, our work may well survive into the future, and shape how people think about the past after we have gone. So we have multiple audiences for our work. But who, primarily, are we working for: ourselves? Our students? Our readers? Before we begin to try and answer these questions, let us go back one stage further and ask: but why *these questions*? Why should we start here?

The last fifty years or so has seen a remarkable amount of activity—written words, spoken words—as historians and others have reflected at length on what they do and how they do it. The imperative for this has in part come from within, and in part from without. Sometimes it has been welcomed, and at others times it has been resisted, and so it has been both an incredibly fertile and fractious time to be a historical practitioner. This period of sustained reflection has done two things. Firstly, it has caused practicing historians to consider deeply the essentials of their discipline in order to refine their thinking and expand the scope of what they do. Secondly, in being forced to confront some of the core methodological assumptions which have underpinned the discipline since the early nineteenth century, historians have been rethinking and reimagining their discipline in quite serious and interesting ways. This is not to understate the depth and intensity of some of the disputes within the historical profession. But overall this has been a fruitful time to be an historian. Yet amidst the blizzard of words, the questions of why we do what we do, and for whom we do it, remain largely hidden. So how did we come to ask ourselves these questions? And what answers did we come up with? Two things prompted this: a question and a death. Let us look at both briefly.

Our starting point came from a foundational question posed by William Katerberg. He argued that perhaps the starting point for the historian who wishes to apply theological ideas and themes to the study of the past should be to ask one simple question, "Who is my neighbor?"[3] Katerberg writes,

> To write history that serves life, that is authentically Christian and meaningfully postmodern, perhaps Christian historians ought to start with a question: "Who is my neighbor?" This is a specifically Christian question, one that does not point to a distinctive Christian methodology, but to a kind of moral imperative that opens scholarship to the wider world. It is also a postmodern question, one that reflects the many traumas and uncertain promise of the twentieth century. It does not seek the closure of objective knowledge, but the indefinite, endless obligations of citizenship, both human and divine.[4]

This is a troubling question because it is so foundational. Who are we, really? And who do we work for? Who are the others in our professional lives as well as our personal lives? However, as we will see, if we take this question as our starting point, it has profound implications for the study of the past. It has the potential to transform not only what we do, but also *how* we do it, why we do it, and for whom we do it. Inexorably, it impinges on both our methodology and also what we produce at the end.

What follows is told by Mark and is based upon his experiences, hence the shift from "we" to "I."

This general question—"who is my neighbor?—was brought into sharp relief by my current research. I am looking at the experience of the Moldavian partisans during World War II under Romanian rule from 1941 to 1944. This research project provided me—Mark, that is—with my

---

3. Katerberg, "Is There Such a Thing?," 57–66.
4. Katerberg, "Is There Such a Thing?," 66.

Death of a Guardsman

"Metzian moment"—when my personal and my professional lives intersected, causing me to pause and ask myself some deeply uncomfortable questions about who I was and why I was doing this work anyway. Two things collided. Two deaths in fact. In my personal life, I was working in the shadow of the recent, unexpected, and rather traumatic death of my mother. Due to a variety of peculiar circumstances I was unable to attend the funeral. This forced me to consider the question: How do you care for the dead when you are absent from them? I encountered the second death in the archival materials I was working on. As I was researching the stories of the Moldavian partisans I came across this short message:

> TOP SECRET
>
> November 1943
>
> To: Comrade Salogor (Central Committee of the Communist Party of Moldavia)
>
> From: Central HQ of the Partisan Movement
>
> According to information supplied to the Central HQ of Partisan Movement, it is known that:
>
> Due to the train crash—which occurred 15/11/43 between Rudnitsa and Kryizhopol'—the train guard Sokol'nik was executed by the Romanians and arrests were made in Noviye and Stariye Popelyukhi.[5]

I carried on working for a while. Later that day my mind started to drift back to this guard. Something about this little incident began to gnaw away at me. Who was he? Why was he executed? How did he die? And what should I do with this little incident? So I went back to the document and looked at it for a while, turned it over in my hands and turned it over in my mind. Questions about this man filled my mind. But then a more troubling question appeared. Why did I move on so quickly? After all, this was the death—and a violent death at that—of another human being. But it failed to register with me. This was troubling. This failure to register was perfectly understandable on one level: I was reading about the occupation of Soviet Moldavia during World War II; people were dying all the time. What made this person so special? I had to keep going because my big project was waiting. Pressures of time, judgments of significance, pragmatic decisions. But

---

5. Socio-Political Archives of the Republic of Moldova (AOSPRM) Fond 3280 Opis 1 Delo 3 p.11.

my answers still proved unsatisfactory. Pragmatic considerations could not alter the fact that my actions felt deeply inhuman, uncaring, calculating, dismissive, thoughtless, heartless. A bit too *professional*. Detached. Clinical. What difference, then, might asking the question: "Who is my neighbor?" make in this situation? Instead of walking away—i.e., carrying on with the research project—the requirement here seemed to be to adopt an other-regarding ethic: What responsibilities does the historian have to the unknown, hidden people who lived before us? Looking at this incident forced me to think about these issues on a more human level. I held a real human being's life and death event in my hands. What should I do with him? Pondering this forged a growing sense of the need to shift the foundational questions and assumptions which underpin the work of the historian, and in particular to think about ways in which we can humanize the study of the past, by reorienting what we do toward human beings: both dead and alive.

What unites historians? In reality, very little. As we mentioned earlier, this has caused historians to default to the lowest common denominator of a commitment to a set of shared practices. This has been in part a response to the growing fragmentation, specialization, and expansion of the discipline. However, this can make us lose sight of the deeply, intrinsically human dimension of everything that we do, and focus instead on refining (and defending) these practices. This myopia toward the human is deepened by the pressures and imperatives caused by the institutional and other structures within which university historians operate: pressures to publish, pressures to get research grants, pressures to specialize, pressures to get rewards and promotion and recognition, and pressures to demonstrate originality. These in turn develop a mentality of utilitarianism toward the past: it can quickly and easily become the vehicle for the pursuit of personal ambitions and agendas. Inexorably, the people of the past often get lost. Overturning this utilitarian attitude means recentering history around human beings, or humanizing our study of the past. As Jeffrey Russell puts it,

> History is the study of the communion of saints—by which I mean the whole flawed failing, loving human race past and present through space and time. The whole point of history and its great joy is to encounter people in the past as real people, to rescue them from oblivion, to restore them as living 4-dimensional people.[6]

---

6. Russell, "Glory in Time," 45.

Death of a Guardsman

Humanizing the study of the past is essentially a process of recovery—our work must recover the idea that got lost somewhere in the move toward becoming a professional, quasi-scientific discipline: that history should serve life, as Nietzsche argues.[7] We need to look carefully at how the structures and practices of the discipline prevent us from valuing the human dimension of our work above all else, and work to recover this sense of moral responsibility in the work of the historian to other human beings. This idea—of history serving life—offers some intriguing possibilities when it comes to helping us to think critically and creatively about what we are doing and why we are doing it. So where do we start in humanizing the past?

What if historians started by thinking about the great mass of dead people out there and asked: *What do we owe the dead?* What if we decide to rethink our approach, and instead seek to place the dead (their needs and rights) at the center of what we do, and why we do it? This is both an intensely moral issue, and also a deeply practical one for historians. Most historians write most of their history most of the time about people who are dead. However, the way we treat the dead often resembles an autopsy carried out on a dead body: we dissect and cut it open so we can find out what we need to know, and then we move on with our research and the body is sewn up, buried, forgotten. Like the practitioner carrying out the autopsy, we stand over the body, work on the body, clinically, coldly, efficiently. We use the dead to prove our hypothesis, or win an argument, or develop a new line of thought, or clarify our understanding. But it is in the main a rather cold process.

Modern Western society often seeks to separate us from the dead, to remove them from our consciousness as we chase the dream of immortality.[8] We push the cemeteries as far away as possible. The dead lie, marginalized, separated from each other and from us. Alone. In 1912, the municipal authorities in San Francisco refused to bury any more of the dead—the cemeteries were overflowing and new land was on prime real estate—so the dead were shipped out. Kicked out. Sent to the local town of Colma which now has 1,600 living residents and 1.5 million deceased residents.[9] This

---

7. See "On the Advantage and Disadvantage of History for Life," in *Untimely Meditations*.

8. The human quest for immortality and the current obsession with trying to realize it is explored in Yuval Noah Harari's work *Homo Deus*.

9. Branch, "Town of Colma," para. 3.

treatment of the dead and the dying around us in the West seems to mirror our treatment of the dead of the past too in some ways.

Today we deny the processes of aging and dying, and ignore the dead and what they might say to us. But this has not always been so, and indeed is not the case in lots of parts of the world today. In other, older times, the dead seemed to be ever-present, especially in times of crisis, such as the Black Death of 1348 to 1350.

FIGURE 7

The dead shadowed the living. Close. Real. Ever-present.

The Ossario di San Martino is a small chapel which houses over 1,200 skulls and over 2,000 bones of soldiers who had originally been buried in mass graves. In other places too, the dead are viewed differently: "The departed person in Africa is not dead and removed from this life, but rather continues to be consciously affirmed in the family as the values, wisdom and example of that person are incorporated into the family."[10]

So what if we began our quest to humanize the study of the past with the dead, and then worked from there? The physical remains of the dead survive (although it is not always known where they reside). Each society has developed elaborate rituals and practices to ensure that the physical

10. Hudson, *Discovering Our Spiritual Identity*, 56.

remains of the person are properly and appropriately dealt with. The corpse is buried or cremated. Complex funeral customs and rites express the diverse beliefs and practices that societies hold in dealing with the dead person. Many of the dead have left us artifacts to hold or gaze upon. Memories of the recent dead still live on in our consciousness, family stories, letters, photographs, on tape or disc, or, increasingly, in "the cloud." Stories and folklore persist. Archaeological remains of settlements and homes and families and burials surround us. The life that was lived by the corpse is dealt with much less systematically though.

But what if we were to try and recover the life that they lived? How do we do that? There is this problem—summarized by Rowan Williams—of the "sheer dreadful irreducible distance" between the living and the dead.[11] Secondly, how might we then take care of the lives they led in ways that are kind and compassionate and not self-serving? How do we show love to these dead people without making them serve our purposes, or use them for our scholarly ends? Beth Barton Schweiger sums this up brilliantly when she writes

> Limited knowledge of the dead is compounded by a second problem, that of the stunning imbalance of power between the historian and subject. I can use the people I encounter in the archives without their consent for my own purposes, for my own pleasures, for my own professional gain. The dead can languish without defense in my books; I can even silence them with their own words. My purposes may be honest. But what if they are not? And what if my honest purposes only end by disfiguring my subjects?[12]

It is precisely at this juncture that historians should begin their work: *What can be done for the lives of the dead?*

Responsibilities to the Dead

Historians should consider carefully our responsibilities to the dead, even as we walk and work among the living. This is not in itself a new way of thinking (of course), but rather a reminder to recover what we may have lost. There are a number of ways in which historians have approached their work from this starting point of the responsibilities we have to the dead.

---

11. Williams, *Ray of Darkness*, 8. Cited in Schweiger, "Seeing Things," 61.
12. Schweiger, "Seeing Things," 61.

One of the first was Jules Michelet, the great French historian of the nineteenth century. Considerations of space make it impossible to do justice to the incredible scope and complexity of Michelet's thinking, so a few observations will have to suffice here.[13] Michelet's work in the *Archives Nationale* in Paris was driven by a project of national popular exhumation. He wanted to restore to life the dead and forgotten masses of French history who had struggled long for justice, equality, and the triumph of the French nation.[14] This act of resurrection, of breathing life into the dead, was the great responsibility of history and the historians:

> Yes, everyone who dies leaves behind a little legacy, his memory, and demands that we care for it. For those who have no friends, the magistrate must provide that care. For the law, or justice, is more certain than all our tender forgetfulness, our tears so swiftly dried. This magistracy is History. And the dead are, to use the language of Roman Law, those *miserabiles personae* with whom the magistrate must preoccupy himself. Never in my career have I lost sight of that duty of the historian.[15]

Thus for Michelet, the duty of the historian was the care and protection of the forgotten people of the past: the poor, the unknown, the invisible, the silent. For Jacques Ranciere, this was not really a moral, paternalistic gesture, but was done for two reasons. One, to fill a yawning void in historical knowledge; the lives of thousands and thousands were unknown, and this had to be addressed. And two, it was also part of the democratic project of nineteenth-century France. By showing that the dead had an important place in the past of France, it affirmed their significance to the political present in France.[16] Ranciere's reading of Michelet seems to echo the approach of Johann Baptist Metz, and also the ideas of Walter Benjamin, who in his theses on history calls upon the historian to brush "against the grain of history" by focusing upon the vanquished and the oppressed rather than the victors.[17] In other words, the responsibilities to the dead of Michelet and others were to the forgotten dead, founded on a political project in the present.[18]

13. Steedman, "'Something She Called a Fever,'" 17–37.
14. White, "Foreword," xvii–xix.
15. Steedman, *Dust*, 39.
16. Steedman, *Dust*, 146, 151.
17. White, "Foreword," ix.
18. Benjamin, "On the Concept of History."

Edith Wyschogrod writes about our responsibilities toward the dead within the context of working on the Shoah. Wyschogrod also occupies a moral standpoint in writing about the responsibilities of the historian in their telling of the past. She describes this as a prior commitment, that is, a responsibility which precedes the practice of narrative construction. She writes that

> the responsibility of the historian is not only to present to future generations but also to those who are absent, who cannot speak for themselves, whose actual faces the historian may never see yet to whom she or he must, as it were, "give face" . . .The historian who assumes liability for the dead feels the pressure of an ethics that is prior to historical judgement. Historical narratives cannot avoid depicting the past for that, after all, is the historian's task. Yet when description is applied to the dead other something is missing, left out, something in the end that cannot be stated in the language of description. . .the other who cannot speak for her—or him—self has a meaning prior to the meanings that are conferred upon her or his behavior, prior to the events belonging to a milieu of the past.[19]

Wyschogrod is at pains to point out the importance of trying to name both the nameless dead and those who have been designated a name by a powerful "other." Namelessness breaks the links of memory and consigns them to oblivion. The historian must restore those broken links. The name becomes, in Wyschogrod's eyes, an "ethical placeholder" or a way in which "she or he makes a person or group come to life."[20] Naming the invisible or insignificant dead becomes a way of restoring or repairing a damaged identity.[21]

Another approach which takes seriously the responsibilities to the dead has been outlined by Antoine de Baets, who argues that historians must work with this in mind as they do their research and writing. He argues that, "Historians study the living and the dead. If we can identify the rights of the living and their responsibilities to the dead, we may be able to formulate a solid ethical infrastructure for historians."[22] De Baets comes from a different place, and his approach is rooted in the language

---

19. Wyschogrod, "Shoah and the Historian's Passion," 30.
20. Wyschogrod, "Shoah and the Historian's Passion," 32.
21. Ryan, Review of *Damaged Identities*, 234–37.
22. de Baets, "Declaration on the Responsibilities," 130.

and discourse of human rights and responsibilities. The argument put forward by de Baets is powerful and compelling. We, the living, have a basic human responsibility to the dead, to treat them with dignity and respect. This general responsibility to the dead encompasses a range of things such as treating the physical remains with integrity, providing an appropriate funeral and burial, respecting their will, recording their death, protecting their reputation and privacy, and so on, what de Baets terms "body and property-related responsibilities" and "personality responsibilities."[23] However, there are also a set of specific responsibilities that pertain to the work of historians, archaeologists, and all those responsible for working with the dead. The role of this latter group is distinctive because the responsibility of historians and others is a systematic universal one to all the dead of history (not the specific responsibilities of relatives). The universal nature of this responsibility poses two dilemmas for historians, though.

The first is a moral question: Should we apply the same standards to all? Do we have the same responsibility to all dead people? Or are we entitled to make some moral judgements about their life? Does the mass murderer/tyrant/terrorist/dictator/criminal (pick your own villain) deserve the same treatment as those who may have led a more virtuous or less problematic life? De Baets argues that universal rules apply: everyone is included, irrespective of the life they have led. All are humans. All deserve the same dignity and respect. The second issue is one of historical universalism: the passage of time creates problems in dealing with the dead, as do the relative levels of knowability. It is relatively straightforward to deal with the recent dead (be they well known or not). Our world keeps extensive records of people, and on the whole it is possible to ensure that the dead in most societies can be remembered and protected. However, the farther back we go, the more difficult it is to deal with the dead. This difficulty is less with the rich, powerful, and famous from the past, who had the means and resources to ensure a legacy and memory was left. It is much trickier to deal with the "anonymous" dead: that great cloud of humanity that has barely left a trace for us to examine. But this "fragile knowability"[24] should not erode the responsibility we have to deal with them as best we can, and with dignity and respect. We need to be aware of the deafening silence that billions of dead people have created and ponder that silence carefully. What can it tell us? First, how we treat the dead should be uppermost in our

---

23. de Baets, "Declaration on the Responsibilities," 144.
24. de Baets, "Declaration on the Responsibilities," 141.

thinking and working. Second, not only do we have a set of responsibilities to the dead, we also have responsibilities to the living. There is an inescapably social and public role of the historian to help people remember, to stop people forgetting, to speak truth to power, to reveal that which has been hidden, to comfort, console, and disturb. We should be concerned about justice, both then and now. Historians have a significant responsibility in building human solidarity across time and space. We seek to bring to life those in the past who have been forgotten, silenced, marginalized, ignored, and oppressed. In so doing we connect them with people in the present, and try to ensure their lives—however short or tragic—are remembered. As we wrestle with the fragile knowability of the untold numbers who have died, we remind ourselves of the stories of untold millions in our world today. We find the stories of hope, courage, betrayal, sacrifice, and persistence, and tell them to our audiences too, that we not only remember, but also go and do likewise: *History that serves life*. De Baets shows us how an orientation centered on human beings—both dead and alive—can reconfigure how and why we do our work. It also raises a different set of questions to guide us in our work: what we study, how we write, and so on.

Hesed, or What Can We Do for the Dead?

There is a related but different approach though: the notion of *Hesed shel emet*. I stumbled across this when reading about the David Irving trial.[25] David Irving was a far right-wing British historian, specializing in Hitler. In 1993, Deborah Lipstadt, an American academic, labeled Irving a spokesperson for Holocaust denial in her book *Denying the Holocaust: the Growing Assault on Truth and Memory*.[26] Irving wanted to restore his reputation and so he sued Lipstadt for libel. At the end of the trial, the judge found in favor of Lipstadt and Penguin books. The details of the trial need not concern us here. However, in a moving reflection after the trial, Lipstadt recounted some of the letters she received from people commending her for taking a stance against Irving and his lies:

> For a long time after the court battle was over, I felt pain when I thought of the many people who had watched Irving ravage their memories. I could not fathom what it felt like to have one's

---

25. There has been a lot written about the Irving Trial. See for example, Lipstadt, *History on Trial*; Evans, *Telling Lies about Hitler*.

26. Lipstadt, *Denying the Holocaust*.

> experiences not just denied, but deprecated and ridiculed. However I felt not just pain, but also a certain sense of privilege. I was reminded of the fact that Jewish tradition highly values acts of loving-kindness, including visiting the sick, sheltering the needy, feeding the hungry and welcoming the stranger. There is however one act of loving-kindness that supersedes all the others because it cannot be reciprocated. Taking care of the dead is called *hesed shel emet*, the most genuine act of loving-kindness, because it is then that we most closely emulate God's kindness to humans, which also cannot be reciprocated. For 5 years I had the privilege to do *hesed shel emet*, to stand up for those who did not survive or who could not stand up for themselves. Being able to do that was thanks enough.[27]

Two things are notable about this passage. Firstly, that Lipstadt felt pain when she considered how the memories of the dead were being treated. It was an emotional response. Secondly, that it was a privilege afforded her to be able to help. Pain and privilege. Standing up for those who could not. This seems to encapsulate something important about the role and the motivation of the historian in doing their work.

So, how might the idea of *Hesed* impact how we do history? Let's unpack the idea a little first, as it has been elaborated upon within Jewish thought and culture. The origins lie in a passage in the book of Genesis:

> When the time drew near for Israel to die, he called for his son Joseph and said to him, "If I have found favor in your eyes, put your hand under my thigh and promise that you will show me kindness and faithfulness. Do not bury me in Egypt, but when I rest with my fathers, carry me out of Egypt and bury me where they are buried." "I will do as you say," he said.[28]

This passage—and in particular this idea of *Hesed*—came to have both a narrow and a broad sense. In its narrow sense, it stood for the idea of ensuring a proper burial for our loved ones. The imperative to treat the dead with the utmost dignity arose from the idea that the body was created by God and was the dwelling place of the soul. This act—of loving care of the dead body and dignity for the dead person—was deemed to be the closest act of kindness a human being could do, because there was no way that it could be repaid by the beneficiary. The impossibility of reciprocation

---

27. Lipstadt, *History on Trial*, 289–90.
28. Gen 47:29–30 (NIV).

meant that the act of *Hesed* was described as most like the loving-kindness expressed by God, which also could not be reciprocated.

Consequently, scholars and theologians began to elaborate upon and amplify the meaning of *Hesed*, extending beyond an act shown toward the dead to include acts of true loving-kindness shown toward the living too. In order to fulfill the criteria of *Hesed* (a special category of loving-kindness if you will), the following requirements have to be present (cited in full from Katherine Doob Sakenfeld):

1. *Hesed* always involves persons.
2. *Hesed* is a specific action, but from a series of such actions the term may also be abstracted to refer to an attitude that is given concrete shape in such actions.
3. The help of another is essential: the person in need cannot perform the action, and the help itself is essential.
4. The circumstances dictate that one person is uniquely able to provide the needed assistance, there is no ready alternative if help is not forthcoming from this source.
5. The person in need has no control over the decision of the person who is in a position to help and there are no legal sanctions for failure to provide help, often no one else will ever know of a negative decision.
6. The potential helper must make a free moral decision, based essentially on commitment to the person in need.
7. *Hesed* focuses the rationale for actions on the commitment to the other, not on advantage to the actor.[29]

Hesed, then, has become something much bigger and wider than a specific set of actions relating to the burial of a loved one: it encompasses an attitude toward others in need (both living and dead) which becomes embodied in a series of actions. In this way, it offers intriguing possibilities when applied to the discipline of history, and to the duties and responsibilities of the historian. If we start to think carefully about how the above criteria might be applied to the study of the past, then its applicability for historians immediately becomes apparent:

---

29. Sakenfeld, *Meaning of Hesed*, 10–11.

- Most of the dead in human history have no one to help them
- The historian is uniquely positioned to provide the necessary assistance; no one else is likely to be able to assist
- There is no compulsion or sanction if the historian does not provide the assistance
- No one will know if the historian decides to move right past the person in need

But why should the historian do this?

Well, to begin with because they can, and they are best placed and best qualified to do so. There must be a moral responsibility that historians have as human beings to take care of those who can do nothing for themselves. In particular, *Hesed* provides a means by which to overcome the damaging utilitarianism that can easily seep into the work of the historian. Instead of us using the past (and for the past here read: dead human beings) for our own ends—whatever they may be, personal or political or ideological or material—we commit ourselves to asking what can we do for the dead, not what can they do for us. We occupy a privileged position (in all sorts of senses). With the privilege comes responsibility. *Hesed* offers us a way to rethink why we do this, and for whom we do it. A new sense of a shared purpose for historians might help us to move beyond intractable disputes over questions of methodology, especially if we begin from a universal position centered on two key aspects of our common humanity: life and death, the living and the dead. This might help us to restore an other-centered ethic to the heart of what we do. This might help us to reimagine what we do in interesting ways. This might help us to connect people across time and space. So how then might *Hesed* affect how we do history? Let us sketch (in outline) what this might look like at a very general level, and then at a more concrete level by revisiting our dead guardsman.

Hesed: The Dignity of the Dead

So what does it mean for the historian to show loving-kindness to the dead? At the center of this approach is the idea of human dignity, or the dignity of the human person. Recognizing and working to uphold the dignity of human beings who are now dead will cause historians to think carefully and compassionately about what we do and why we do it. This will pose challenges for the historian, without doubt. The aspiration to establish the human dignity of the dead in history will mean different things for different people in different contexts, but it seems to me that five stand out as being worthy of note (there are others obviously). In particular, we need to save or rescue the dead from the following scenarios:

1. Invisibility or "fragile knowability"
2. Historical imprecision or the abhorrence of "about"
3. Overfamiliarity or the assumed truth
4. Vilification or the judgment of the present
5. The contestations of ideology and/or ethnicity

Let us take these in turn.

1. The Problem of Invisibility

Perhaps the greatest challenge lies in how the historian has to deal with the great cloud of unknown or hardly known people who have lived throughout history. There are numerous reasons why they may be unknown: the absence of written records, a premature death, or just sheer unremarkableness. They grew up, worked, lived, and then died. No one thought to keep a record of their life, their thoughts, their deeds. They did not keep a record themselves. No pictures. No letters. Nothing. Invariably these will be the poor and the uneducated, the ordinary folk of history. The rich and famous and powerful will find ways to have their lives and memories preserved and their legacy established. Yet for the poor and the ordinary, no such facility exists. They remain silent, silenced, ignored, marginalized. How can we make them visible? How can we, even though they are dead, give them life again? How can we know anything? How do we decide whom to choose? *Hesed* should compel us to try and remove this cloak of invisibility and begin to think about how best to grapple with the fragile knowability of this cloud of people who have passed on, to ensure we remember, we see, we make them present even though the body is absent. For we must remember that invisibility is not the same as insignificance. Graham Swift remarks on this in *Waterland*:

> And did I not bid you remember, children, that for each protagonist who once stepped onto the stage of so-called historical events, there were thousands, millions who never entered the

theatre—who never knew that the show was running—who got on with the donkey work of coping with reality? True, true. But it doesn't stop there. Because each one of those numberless non-participants was doubtless concerned with raising in the flatness of his own unsung existence his own personal stage, his own props and scenery. . . .[30]

The problem of invisibility and trying to recover the lives of those lost is brilliantly depicted by Rachel Whiteread's *Judenplatz* Holocaust memorial: a sealed library of closed books, each book suggesting a whole life we cannot recover.

FIGURE 8

One of the drastic losses that modernity has brought has been to separate the living and the dead, to make the dead invisible, to eliminate them from our consciousness. In a brilliant series of theses, John Berger has reflected "On the Economy of the Dead." In his twelfth and final thesis, he notes:

> How do the living lie with the dead? Until the dehumanization of society by capitalism, all the living awaited the experience of the dead. It was their ultimate future. By themselves the living were incomplete. Thus living and dead were interdependent. Always. Only a uniquely modern form of egotism has broken this

30. Swift, *Waterland*, 34.

interdependence. With disastrous results for the living, who now think of the dead as *eliminated*.[31]

Hesed helps us not only to remove the invisibility cloak, but to reverse the processes of elimination and restore the interdependence between the living and the dead. In the book of Hebrews in the Bible, it talks about the people of God being surrounded by a "great cloud of witnesses" compressing the distance between the present and the past, the living and the dead, and showing why the living need the dead. We need each other.

2. *The Problem of Imprecision*

How do we address the imprecise human accounting of the mass killings of modernity? This last point I stumbled across recently when I read the poem by Zbigniew Herbert, "Mr Cogito on the Need for Precision," in *Report from the Besieged City and Other Poems*.[32] This poem pleads with us to counter ignorance and indifference about those who have disappeared, to work against imprecision in historical accounting. Herbert notes that we use the shameful word "about" when we talk about the multiplicity of human victims of mass murder, accidents, or warfare. But such imprecision about dead humans is unacceptable and callous, for every single dead person matters.

3. *The Problem of Overfamiliarity*

And then there are those at the other end of the spectrum, the ones we seem to know only too well. We have read about them, heard about them. Their historical reputation precedes them. This can lead to two problems. The first is a lack of attention. If we assume that there is very little more to be said about an individual, then historians will tend to move on to other more interesting or more fashionable topics or people. The second is iconoclasm. Historians often decide that because there seems to be a well-established reputation, this should be challenged or debunked. So the historian turns iconoclast. They seek to tear down the historical reputation and reveal the "real" person. They come to reveal truth, contest hagiography, bludgeon myth, and peer through nostalgia. In either case, the human being gets lost,

---

31. Berger, "On the Economy," 32.
32. Herbert, *Report from the Besieged City*.

encased in the reputation or broken in the act of iconoclasm. *Hesed* should cause us to pause and search again for the person.

4. *The Problem of Vilification, or the Judgment of the Present*

Some people, it seems, have a universal sense of condemnation resting upon them. The evil dictator, the SS guard, the brutal amoral revolutionaries, the evil settler-colonist, the priests overseeing human sacrifices, the ruthless POW camp commandant, the heartless slave trafficker, the fickle monarch, the racist missionary, the eugenics scientist—people in the past who, through a series of actions associated with them, are now subject to the judgment of the historian, to vilification after having done the indefensible. How then does *Hesed* deal with this issue? *Hesed* has to confront what has been done, especially if it involves inflicting pain and suffering and misery upon the powerless, the weak, the poor. Loving-kindness has to be extended to all. It cannot whitewash or make excuses. But it has to be offered to all: victims and perpetrators. The guilty and the innocent. When we handle the lives of those who have been vilified and condemned, what can we say? Do we allow the unspeakable acts(s) to define them, or do we attempt to re-humanize them? *Hesed* must cause us to look through or peer behind the vilification. And this is not just an act of contextualization, a seeking to understand why they did X or Y (although that might have to happen too). No, if we go down that road we are already defining them completely by the thing that we deplore. We have to find out who they are. *Hesed* will not define someone in such a crude, one-sided way.

5. *The Problem of Contestation*

Finally, for now, the problem of those figures who deeply divide opinion. As history has expanded, become more plural and more global, so the number of voices involved in making it has grown. History is a seemingly never-ending series of interpretations and reinterpretations of key events and phenomena and individuals. New interpretations come along and supplant old ones, or synthesize different opinions. Historians set up camps, defend their opinions, attack those of their opponents. This is the landscape of revisionism and revisionist history, whereby historians are constantly in the process of revising the story, retelling it, or telling it anew. This is seen as part of the health of the discipline: a healthy posture of questioning everything. This creates great divides amongst historians over how they interpret both key events—the origins of World War I or the cause of the fall of Rome or the Cold War—and some of history's key contested figures—Robespierre, Thatcher, Churchill, Lenin, Tamerlane, Ataturk—and so on. How does *Hesed* deal with these contested views? How can we rescue those who are deeply contested? What does loving-kindness look like when opinion is so polarized, so seemingly irreconcilable?

Hesed offers us the opportunity to try and recover the humanity of the people who have died, a humanity which will undoubtedly be rich, contradictory, troubling, mundane, uplifting, and puzzling. It should help us to prevent some of the excessive utilitarian and functional approaches to the past. It should make us question what we read, and it should make us sensitive to nuance and context. It is, in many ways, an attempt by historians to answer the question "Who is my neighbor?" By serving the dead who cannot help themselves, we write history that serves life.

Let's go back to our guardsman, and to the dilemma of how to deal with his premature, violent, untimely death. How might *Hesed* help us here (the "invisibility" category outlined above)? There is no one satisfactory answer, for the very issue that causes us to pause is the very one that defeats us: we just don't know very much about this individual. There is no physical description. There is nothing about how old or tall he is, his marital status, his family background, never mind his personality, his likes and dislikes, his fears and anxieties, his beliefs and values. What made him laugh? Where did he live? What did he think of the war? He might have been loving and kind. He might have been cruel and vindictive. We just don't know. But that does not mean we cannot proceed. Here are some practices we might plausibly explore.

1. *Remember the Dead*

One of the constant pressures that weighs on scholars of all disciplines is the pressure of time, and the pressure to publish. This causes people to work with undue haste, rushing through research, hurrying to get to where they need to be. The idea of pausing and stopping in the midst of all this activity to remember a person or persons—whom we do not know and will probably never know—is rather counterintuitive. But this is really the first and most important step. We need to stop, pause our journey, and cross over to where the body lies. In doing this we begin to discipline ourselves through this action to give expression to the principle of *Hesed*. *Hesed* only becomes meaningful when it compels us to reorient our priorities and begin to do things differently and do different things. *Hesed* recognizes that this person matters. Their death is not just another death in a long line of deaths. It confronts the seeming finality of physical death and enforces a silent pause. At that particular moment, nothing is more important. We stop the march of time. We make ourselves recall this person, bring them back to life, even for a moment.

The act of stopping, pausing, remembering, and tending to the dead person can be seen as a mere gesture, lacking substance. But this, I think, is to understate the power of small gestures and the potential inherent in every act of remembrance to subvert the present state of things, with its emphasis upon outcomes and deadlines and impact in our work. Instead, by remembering one of the great cloud of unknown, unheralded, insignificant people from the past, we declare something radically different: that there is another way of working which seeks to dignify all those who have gone before us. Remembering itself becomes an action replete with meaning, for in remembering this person we rescue them from the anonymity of statistical collation or from being defined merely as a victim (one from the roll call of victims of war or disease or execution) or from the mass of invisible people who left little record or trace. In our tiny acts of remembering, we stand silent and still, we allow these ghosts a life and a voice and invite them to speak to us.

Hesed then must compel us to stop and remember the dead. In doing so, we not only restore their humanity, but we also bring meaning to their suffering. In doing so, we disturb the certainties of our own present and this becomes an act of listening as well as remembering. As we remember their lives, we listen and invite them to speak.

2. *Gathering the Fragments*

Stopping, pausing, and remembering is only the start though. When we stumble across the fragile remnants of someone's life, we have to gather up these fragments. As historians they have been entrusted to us. We have a duty of care. The fragments are just that: broken, random, haphazard, frail. They are susceptible to loss, decay, destruction. It must be a deliberate act on our part to gather them up, rescue them, and in so doing save them, so that they might bear witness.

A couple of examples. Oradour-sur-Glane is a small village in France which in 1944 was subject to a Nazi atrocity. All the residents were rounded up and shot. After the war, the French authorities decided not to rebuild the village but to leave it in its ruined state as a permanent testimony to those who died. It requires maintenance, of course. But it stands—broken, ruined, haunting—as a testimony to the atrocities of Nazism, and to all those who perished there. The village could easily have been rebuilt. The old buildings which witnessed the atrocities could have been pulled down and a new village built, along with appropriate memorials, shrines, and other *aides-memoire*. But the authorities decided the fragments themselves were too valuable, that they told such an important story that they should stand as they were. Broken, ruined, incomplete. Yet they haunt us.[33]

There is also a project entitled "Gathering the Fragments"[34] organized by Yad Vesham as part of their Holocaust Remembrance project.

> During the Shoah, an entire world was shattered. The remaining scattered fragments vary infinitely in size, shape and texture—from documents to diaries, testimonies to artifacts, photographs to works of art. Despite their wide dispersion, they can still be found in many places—government and private archives, libraries, and even in the homes of people who went through the vortex of the Shoah, and members of their families left behind. Each fragment tells its own tale and, like a thread, has a beginning and an end. These threads of information, intersecting and combining, are then woven together into a broad and deep tapestry that depicts a multifaceted story stretching over time and space. In this way we can reconstruct as much of the shattered Jewish world as possible, the events that led to its destruction, and the lives that continued to be lived while the devastation unfolded. Since its inception, Yad Vashem has strived to collect every relevant source of information, each of which enlightens us in its own unique way about the six million Jews murdered and the millions more persecuted and victimized during the Holocaust. Yet some shards remain locked in the memories of those who were there, still waiting to be expressed in word or art. Others languish in desk or dresser drawers, in old suitcases, or in shoeboxes. And some are precious, kept close to the heart and seldom shown to others. The fragments we collect have universal meaning for us as human beings, national meaning for us as Jews, and often very personal meaning as well.[35]

33. The official website of Oradour, which explains the purpose of the memorial, can be found here: http://www.oradour.info/. The notice at the entrance to the ruins says *Souviens toi* (Remember!).

34. See: http://www.yadvashem.org/gathering-fragments.

35. Rozett, "Gathering the Fragments," para. 1.

This process of gathering fragments—however small, frail, or solitary they may be—has great significance. The fragments themselves are unique testimonies to a life. Together they form a bigger mosaic, interconnected and interwoven, testifying to some universal themes in human history and connecting us tangibly to these "invisibles." Our actions in collecting fragments—be they artifacts or testimonies or snippets of the life—demonstrate a posture of utmost care, lest these things be lost forever. If we do not gather these fragments—the only things we can know—then who will? My own work in *Gathering the Fragments* involves a blog I have started entitled *Sandgrains in Infinity*. As I come across stories or snippets or names in the documents I read, I have resolved to write about them, and in this way gather the fragments of people's lives so that they might not be lost.[36]

3. *The Spaces Between*

So we remember. We gather. But a third way exists. Between the fragments are a great multitude of spaces. This great swathe of unknown spaces between the fragments can only really be dealt with through imagination and narration, if we wish to deal with them, that is. We do not know much about our guardsman. There are so few details. Faced with this, one avenue to go down is to narrate his life into being. This approach can be seen in the stunning collection of stories *The Things They Carried*, written by Tim O'Brien, which reflect upon the Vietnam experience (and also upon the art and craft of storytelling itself).[37] Visceral, absorbing, uncomfortable, and challenging, O'Brien uses fiction to open up truths about Vietnam, to make us feel the lived experience of combat, loss, camaraderie, cruelty, indifference, courage, and cowardice. O'Brien delves deep into the power of story, and its ability both to save us and to bring life back to the dead, because "in a story, which is a kind of dreaming, the dead sometimes smile and sit up and return to the world. . .we kept the dead alive with stories."[38] This can be the act of *Hesed* for the dead. We cannot resurrect the body. But we can reanimate the life. Tell stories, imagine. Dream about the guardsman's life. Not because we wish to sate our desire for accurate knowledge about him. Not because we want to reconstruct his life, his struggles, his demise, but because we can give him life once more, let him live, let him mean again.

36. See: https://wordpress.com/posts/sandgrainsblog.wordpress.com.
37. O'Brien, *Things They Carried*.
38. O'Brien, *Things They Carried*, 225, 239.

As we narrate him, we put flesh on his bones. We make him present. If we narrate these spaces between the fragments, the spaces of unknowingness, then absence can become presence.

4. To Name or to Be Silent?
The Dilemma of Violence, Silence, Narratives, and Counterstories

The idea of using narratives about the lives of the insignificant, the invisible, the unimportant, or those with "fragile knowability," is not without problems though. In the example above—of narrating the spaces between—we inevitably encounter the issue of narrative vs. accuracy/truth. Which is more important for the historian: to get the story right (even if that means basically not being able to tell it) or to tell a story that contains truth, even if it is not "what actually happened?" In addition, there are those who argue that what we should be showing the dead more than anything is respect: quiet silence. They should be left alone. When we take their lives and shape it into some form of narrative, then we immediately perpetrate another act of symbolic violence upon their life, for we constitute their life again, in a way in which they have no control. Writing a story of their life becomes then an act of violence, ripping apart the tangled threads of their life and creating a new piece of fabric. This act of storying is akin to disturbing the bones: an act of sacrilege, or at worst a type of grave robbing, using the contents of the grave for our own ends.

The counterpoint to this view is that the exercise in writing a "counterstory"—a new narrative of a disempowered, ignored, oppressed, or previously silenced or unheard group or individual—is actually a powerful form of resistance and liberation which restores and repairs their identity and dignity. The act of telling the story is restorative. It is not akin to grave robbing, but is actually closer to finding the remains of the person, and giving them a proper burial for the first time. Multiple testimonies exist of how the act of telling a story—or being listened to properly for the first time—is a deeply emotional empowering act (almost irrespective of the truth claims of the narrative).[39] The key issues then seem to be: "*What type of counterstory is to be told* (not the act itself)?" *and "Who does the telling?"* for quite clearly a narrative can be deeply exploitative, self-serving, and oppressive. Equally it can be liberating and restorative. Here is where I believe *Hesed* can help us, for the motivation—an act of loving-kindness—should help

---

39. Ryan, Review of *Damaged Identities*, 234–35.

us to shape a narrative which is sensitive, which seeks to repair a damaged identity or helps us to know the previously unknown, and above all which compels us to listen.

But there are other questions:

Who does the telling?

Can we tell the story of another?

Should we tell the story of another?

Who owns all these stories anyway?

One more thing. Recent estimates (probably little more than educated guesses) show that there are fifteen dead people for every living human being on earth right now.[40] The act of burial that all societies engage in deals, definitively, with the problem of the cadaver or corpse. But the dead person requires constant concern, care, and attention, and historians can and should do this. The idea of *Hesed* offers us the chance to not only think anew about why we do what we do, but also what we do and how we do it. Amidst indifference and solitude, we have a loving obligation to care for the dead and make them present once again. And maybe loving-kindness toward the dead will transform our practices. Beth Barton Schweiger concludes by noting that

> in the end envisioning love in history is to envision love in the here and now. Seeing the dead affords practice in seeing the living. The limits of our understanding of those who are gone are matched by our blindness toward the people across the room. The limits of our wisdom and charity toward the subjects of our books is matched by the limits of self-giving love in our daily lives.[41]

And so seeing the dead is also an exercise in seeing the living and so loving those around me as well as those in the archives. In being a neighbor to the dead, they show me how to be a neighbor to the living, for we are our neighbor's keeper after all.

---

40. Stephenson, "Do the Dead," para. 22.
41. Schweiger, "Seeing Things," 77.

CHAPTER 6

HISTORY THAT HEALS

We begin this chapter with two apologies, with two pledges to seek healing and reconciliation.

On June 11, 2008, Prime Minister Stephen Harper stood up in Canada's Parliament to deliver a momentous apology on behalf of settler Canadians to Indigenous peoples, and especially to the over 150,000 survivors of Indian residential schools. Assembled in the chamber to hear his words were dozens of Indigenous leaders, survivors, and Canadian dignitaries, and Harper spoke with considerable emotion and feeling. Harper recounted the history of Canada's policies and practices of cultural genocide in its relationship with Indigenous peoples, and outlined how for over a century tens of thousands of Indigenous children had been taken from their homes and sent to state- and church-run residential schools to "Christianize" and "civilize" them. Many died, and many others were physically and sexually abused. The cumulative trauma of this experience as well as the oppressive weight of Canada's long colonial history had been devastating, Harper acknowledged:

> The burden of this experience has been on your shoulders for far too long. The burden is properly ours as a Government, and as a country. There is no place in Canada for the attitudes that inspired the Indian Residential Schools system to ever prevail again. You have been working on recovering from this experience for a long time and in a very real sense, we are now joining you on this journey. The Government of Canada sincerely apologizes and asks the forgiveness of the Aboriginal peoples of this country for failing them so profoundly.

Nous le regrettons
We are sorry
Nimitataynan
Niminchinowesamin
Mamiattugut

And so Harper committed Canadians to a new shared history of healing and reconciliation with the original peoples of the land on which we live and work.[1]

The second apology involves our university, as well as many other participants. Beyond an expansive program of financial compensation, one of Harper's commitments to the survivors of residential schools was to establish a Truth and Reconciliation Commission (TRC) whose task it was to explore the historical roots of Canada's policies of cultural genocide, to set the foundation for a future of reconciliation, healing, and justice, and perhaps most important, to listen—to listen to the stories of suffering and resilience of those women and men whose lives had been devastated when they were taken as children to residential schools by the state and by Christian churches. For five years, the TRC—gracefully led by its commissioners, Murray Sinclair, Wilton Littlechild, and Marie Wilson—toured the country and listened to thousands of stories, testimonies of loss, recovery, anger, and suffering. The TRC also held seven national events, including one in Edmonton in 2014, which our entire university attended. Our university's president, Melanie Humphreys, spoke words of apology and reconciliation on our behalf: "We want to know the truth and we have learned that the truth is painful beyond bearing," she said. "We have listened to the experiences of survivors. We have been moved by their tears, inspired by their courage, and impelled to seek greater understanding of pathways to healing and hope so that we may know how to walk our life-affirming journey together." And, she said, "this is no mere intellectual exercise for us. Our mission is to engage and educate students to become agents of reconciliation and hope."[2] And so our president committed our university to a new shared history of healing and reconciliation with the original peoples of the land on which we live and work.

---

1. Indigenous and Northern Affairs Canada, "Statement of Apology." Read the full statement here: https://www.aadnc-aandc.gc.ca/eng/1100100015644/1100100015649.

2. Humphreys, Melanie. "Expression of Reconciliation." Document in authors' possession.

We do not want to claim any special virtue on the part of our university in making this declaration; hundreds of churches, groups, and institutions made similar pledges throughout the course of the TRC, and we assume (or hope) that these statements were genuine and represent authentic, heartfelt commitments to reconciliation. In fact, our statement requires more analysis about power, representation, and who has the responsibility to speak—or listen. The proof of our authenticity will be in the actions, not in the words. Still, one of the things that is striking to us as Christian historians is the way in which the statement makes an embodied connection between scholarship and justice, because it created a space in which neutrality or disinterestedness toward the past is not an option. This was no mere intellectual exercise, we said; we took a stance on the past that reflected our commitment to a new future.

Our intention in this chapter is to consider what it means, as members of the historical profession and as Christian historians, to place ourselves within the promises of confession, apology, repentance, healing, and advocacy. We will juxtapose the liturgies of the TRC, with its rituals and practices of purposive remembering, with those of the historical profession of which we are a part. And what we want to suggest is that there are subversive and even radical implications at play when we say "I'm sorry."

We will return to the two apologies later in the chapter. First, however, we'll begin with some foundational considerations.

What Does God Require of You?

Christians are called to be peacemakers and to be ministers of reconciliation. We are called to emulate the instructions of the prophet Micah. "What does God require of you?" Micah asks. The answer is disarmingly and perhaps impossibly simple: "To do justice, to love mercy, and to walk humbly with your God."[3] We are called to love God above all, and to love our neighbors as ourselves. We take these imperatives as axiomatic for Christian historians, too. Christian historians must do justice, love mercy, and walk humbly with God.

As academic historians trained and employed in the liturgies of the Western historical profession, we write from the perspective of a discipline whose predisposition is generally tilted against prophetic and/or political

3. Mic 6:8 (NIV).

advocacy. We have diagnosed some of the liturgies and structures that have created those impediments in previous chapters. Our universities—Christian and secular—are increasingly corporatized, prioritizing their role as selling credentials to consumers (students) to plug them usefully into the global capitalist economy rather than forming them for subversive discipleship. For all the triumphalistic talk of progress on social equality in North America since World War II, our universities and history departments (including ours) often still reflect longstanding colonial patterns of racial, class, and gender privilege, discrimination, and inequality. And for all the good the methodological liturgies of the historical profession in the West can do, those same modernist liturgies have been and still are being used in the service of injustice, sexism, colonialism, and racism. Our practices and institutions can be used to silence and erase as easily as they can be used to give voice and to empower.

All scholarship, whether we recognize it or not, is inherently political; it is in advocacy of something. To the question, then, as to whether or not Christian historians ought to be political, our answer is an emphatic yes. Neutrality is not an option. This is implied in our previous chapters, in invoking Metz's concepts of antihistory and dangerous memory as the foundation for particular Christian stances toward the past, and in the practices of *Hesed*, of care for and defense of the dead. This chapter takes those arguments further.

How can Christian historians act as advocates for justice and reconciliation? How can we do history that heals? How might Christian historians be peacemakers? How might we live out the ministry of reconciliation in our work—in our teaching, research, and practices?

The problem with asking such large and complicated questions is that they cannot be answered in the abstract. They cannot be answered universally or generically. Christian historians must act for peace, justice, and reconciliation, yes, but the ways they do so must be particular to the contexts in which they find themselves. We do not propose here a singular formula for liturgies of peace and reconciliation for all Christian historians to follow because such a formula does not exist. Justice is never generic; it is always specific and contextual. Reconciliation is never generic; it is always relational and personal. Theologian John de Gruchy, on whom many of our reflections rely, observes that reconciliation is an action rooted in practices of transforming power. Understood only as theory, reconciliation is simply ahistorical and abstract doctrine; instead, "reconciliation is properly understood as a process in which we become engaged at the heart of the struggle for justice and peace in the world." That is why, he says, "any discussion of reconciliation must be historically and contextually centred."[4] These affirmations have shaped our own reflections on Canada's TRC. We should note here that our reflections might have implications for considering the questions of reconciliation and truth in other contexts (such as the history of white supremacy and American race relations, for example), but our intention here is to be as specific as possible.

Saying Sorry

What does it mean to say "I'm sorry" or "We are sorry" for the sins of the past? All claims to justice and reconciliation must be rooted in the recognition of one party (the one that perpetuated the harm or injustice) that it has done wrong to another. But there are subversive and even radical implications at play when the offender comes to the verge of repentance. It is a powerful thing to apologize, to seek forgiveness and reconciliation, and it is fraught and difficult. It is probably fair to say that everyone knows instinctively that to say sorry is one thing, but an apology unaccompanied by transformed relationships and practices is at best empty words and at worst duplicitous, an act that amplifies or exacerbates the original wrong. In saying sorry, we commit ourselves to a new way of walking with those we have harmed, and we commit ourselves to a new story. We can see apologies as forms of antihistory or dangerous memory because they disrupt the myths or narratives on which we build our societies and our loves. But what's so dangerous about saying sorry?

Most Christians know that confession and repentance are a longstanding and essential part of Christian liturgical practice, of course, one perhaps underemphasized in many contemporary North American evangelical churches. Denominations from more liturgical traditions make confession a central fixture of their collective worship. "We have offended against thy holy laws," the Anglican *Book of Common Prayer* intones; "we have left undone those things which we ought to have done, and we have done those things which we ought not to have done."[5] Roman Catholicism historically has emphasized penance in conjunction with absolution, those

---

4. de Gruchy, *Reconciliation*, 21.

5. *Book of Common Prayer*, Daily Office Morning Prayer, Rite One: https://www.bcponline.org/DailyOffice/mp1.html.

actions in response to the forgiveness of sin that restore the sinner to right relations with God, neighbor, and community. Confession and penance go hand in hand, and both are required for healing. Penance is an essential part of our worship.

If Christians know of the need for penitence before reconciliation, it is only more recently that nation-states, corporations, and even educational institutions have made apologizing for past wrongs a feature of their public obligations. What this relatively new phenomenon means is a complicated question. The editors of a recent book, *The Age of Apology: Facing Up to the Past*, call this the "apology phenomenon," describing what seems to be a historically unprecedented series of state apologies and truth and reconciliation commissions that are driven, the editors claim, by an "almost universal recognition that a society will not be able to successfully pass into the future until it somehow deals with its demons from the past."[6] What editors mean by that, and whether it's true, of course, is another question. But consider how since the end of the Second World War the country of Germany has wrestled with its crime of the Holocaust, and the financial and commemorative practices it has enacted to speak to its guilt. Likewise, many readers will be familiar with South Africa's Truth and Reconciliation Commission that wrestled with that country's history of apartheid, and many other countries—including Canada—have embarked on similar processes of truth-telling and forgiveness for crimes and genocide in their pasts. The United States as a nation, it seems, has been more reluctant to make public declarations of guilt and forgiveness for historical wrongs. Still, whether these national exercises have led to genuine healing, justice, and restoration is also an open question. Corporations, too, make public declarations of apology frequently if their actions or products lead to harm or worse, although we might speculate that they do so for reasons of brand protection, damage control, or to impede lawsuits rather than out of genuine contrition. Some companies, interestingly enough, have extended apologies for actions in the deeper past. In 2000, the American insurance company Aetna apologized for its role in financing and supporting the internal slave trade during the 1850s, though the apology was not accompanied by financial reparations. More recently, educational institutions such as Georgetown University have apologized too. A Jesuit institution, in 1838, Georgetown sold off some of its property—278 enslaved people—to keep itself financially solvent, and in 2017, the school made expansive gestures

---

6. Howard-Hassman and Gibney, "Introduction," 1.

of apology and reconciliation to the descendants of the people it had sold so long ago.[7] In a profound way, Georgetown has begun to rewrite its own history in ways that include institutional transformation. Rightly so, for as theologian Jeremy Bergen tells us, a church or institution or nation "seized by the injustice it has promoted will be called to more than minor adjustments and new programs, but to a radical and ongoing conversion in its common life."[8] *Conversion*—a theological turn toward reconciliation—is a radical, dangerous, and ongoing practice.

The sins of history have very long traces and leave deep scars, but it is sometimes mystifying even to Christians what these apologies mean, what they accomplish, and whether they are even necessary. Some might ask why "we" ought to be held responsible for the sins of "our" ancestors— "we" didn't do anything wrong, after all, "they" did. The past is the past, we might say, and we can't change what happened. The assumption that there is some sort of statute of limitations for historical crimes, that the past should be left alone, is a convenient though perhaps understandable default position or reaction. Or, we might say, it's wrong for us to judge the actions of people in the past through the moral or ethical standards of the present. We think differently today about slavery or colonialism, for example, than most (white) people did two hundred years ago. Who are we to judge our strange ancestors who believed and acted so differently than us? Why do we need to repent for slavery, for colonialism, or for the Crusades, for that matter?

These are deeply complicated questions, and we will pose only two short answers here. The first is the simple point that the past is never past, that the sins of history have set in place continuing patterns and structures of racial, social, and gender inequalities on which, for example, countries like Canada and the United States are built. The second is a particular theological claim for Christians that repentance is an integral vocation of being part of the church, the body of Christ, the communion of saints. At the center of all history and creation stands the risen Christ who reconciles all things—including history—to the triune God. As followers of Christ, we are called to the ministry of repentance and reconciliation. "Within the communion of the saints," says Jeremy Bergen, "forgiveness in Christ is what binds the church together as a single community though time and

---

7. For more on this story, see Georgetown's digital archive of the *Working Group on Slavery, Memory, and Reconciliation*: http://slavery.georgetown.edu/

8. Bergen, *Ecclesial Repentance*, 12.

space." Christian repentance for history as part of the body of Christ "may be understood as an act of the Holy Spirit to constitute the temporal continuity of the church by binding the church and its history of sin to its singular source of forgiveness, and to free the church for its future by granting forgiveness for the sins of its past." Repentance for the past is part of the church's continuing work of holiness, of reformation, and of conversion for the sake of the world.[9]

Theologian John de Gruchy has also written at great length about the Christian theologies and practices of reconciliation from the vantage point of the TRC in South Africa. He observes the paradoxical danger of speaking of reconciliation, of Christians daring "to claim with St. Paul that God was in Christ reconciling the world to himself,'" a conviction, he says, that is at the heart of the Christian tradition.[10] But genuine reconciliation is deeply fraught with all sorts of subjectivities and complexities. How *dare* we speak of reconciliation, he asks? Consider carefully what de Gruchy says here:

> Many voices speak of reconciliation, but what they say depends on who is speaking, on their experience, their location in society, their perception of the past, the audience they are addressing, and the reason why they are speaking. Whose reconciliation is at stake and for what purpose? On whose terms are we seeking to achieve it? Do we speak from a position of power or out of weakness? Who, then, are *we* who dare to speak about reconciliation? Are we speaking for ourselves, on behalf of others, or with others? Who are we listening to before we speak, or are we not listening at all? Hearing the truth from the alienated 'other' is a prerequisite for daring to speak of reconciliation. But is our speech about reconciliation forcing some to remain silent, perhaps nursing grievances or even plotting revenge? The absence of speech is often more significant than its presence. The absence of speech about reconciliation forces us to consider the silence of those who refuse to participate in the discussion and their reason for doing so. Could it be that the good news of reconciliation is simply wishful thinking, a way of escape from the harsh realities of conflict confronting us? Are we speaking about reconciliation in order to forget the past, or in order to deal justly with its legacy? Dare we proclaim such a message if in doing so we reinforce structures of injustice and undermine the will to resist and transformation? Could it be

---

9. Bergen, *Ecclesial Repentance*, 286.
10. de Gruchy, *Reconciliation*, 17.

that the message of reconciliation has become a rhetorical tool in the hands of politicians and preachers combining to prevent the birth of a more just world? In what sense, then, can Christians fulfill their mandate to proclaim the gospel of reconciliation?[11]

Read that quote again, because if de Gruchy's warnings and questions are true for Christians who wish to proclaim the gospel of reconciliation, they are equally true for Christian historians. We will remind you of de Gruchy's warnings at the end of this chapter.

Again, we repeat the assertion, our belief, that faith-based academic historians (and academic institutions) have a responsibility to engage with—and be transformed by—the vital work of reconciliation. How do we remember rightly? How might our practices of remembering and our scholarly liturgies be transformed in the cause of reconciliation? We will argue for immersive and engaged historical practices that contribute to healing, justice, and reconciliation. Instead of adopting a posture of scholarly detachment or assuming that our task is to simply describe the past "as it really happened," Christian historians might instead work to *change* history as agents of healing and hope. But it is important to acknowledge our limitations, too, and to qualify what we mean by changing history. Some wounds are too deep to heal, and some stories are not ours to tell. Historians—Christian or otherwise—must not adopt a salvationist attitude toward the past whereby they see themselves as agents of the world's redemption. Historians, in other words, must not play God.

The TRC in Canada

For the rest of this chapter we will reflect on these ideas and challenges with specific reference to the TRC in Canada, again with the contention that any argument for reconciliation and justice in Christian historical practices must be contextual, relational, and specific, not generic and abstract. This chapter opened with two apologies—one from Prime Minister Harper, who apologized to Indigenous people on behalf of settler Canadians for our national policy of residential schools, and the other from our university president, who committed our university to the task of reconciliation. We will begin by trying to put these apologies into historical context, with the caveat that our brief summary inevitably will be reductive and insufficient.

11. de Gruchy, *Reconciliation*, 16.

Re-Forming History

Readers are encouraged to explore this history further, particularly through the extraordinary resources of the TRC itself.[12]

As a partial reaction to de Gruchy's injunctions (see above), it's actually important that we locate ourselves in relationship to the TRC and the history of cultural genocide that it was charged to explore. Throughout what follows, we identify ourselves, and all Canadians who are not Indigenous, as *settlers*. So what's in a name? On the surface, it may sound like an untroubling term but its usage here has implications that relate directly to the unsettling and even dangerous task of reconciliation. By calling ourselves *settlers,* we are citing our position by locating ourselves as members of the dominant culture which still benefits from centuries of historic (and continuing) colonialism in Canada. We are members of the perpetrating society who enacted residential schools, among many other acts of colonial violence. It will not do to imagine that we can write what follows from a position of neutrality, dispassionate innocence, or lack of complicity. If we are to make any contribution to reconciliation, we have to know who we are and recognize that the risks and vulnerability entailed in reconciliation fall much heavier on those who are not so protected as we are by layers of power and privilege. Emma Battell Lowman and Adam J. Barker (who are settlers themselves) helpfully call the term "settler" an "*interrogative identity*":

> When people identify as Indigenous, they identify with entire histories and creation stories of how they belong on certain lands, with cultural, spiritual, and political practices that are embodied in those stories that connect them to those lands. When we say we are Settler people, we are recognizing that our stories are different, and when we ask others to identify as Settler people, we are likewise asking them: How did you come to be here? How do you claim belonging here? And, most importantly, can we belong in a way that doesn't reproduce colonial dispossession and harm?[13]

They invite settlers into "the space of dangerous freedom"[14] by accepting the story of who we are with the expectation that decolonization and

---

12. See the website for the National Centre for Truth and Reconciliation: http://nctr.ca/map.php.
13. Lowman and Barker, *Settler*, 19.
14. Lowman and Barker, *Settler*, 120.

reconciliation require us to center our identities in new stories. This idea also frames our analysis below.

Here's another troubling and unsettling word: *genocide*. This is how the authors of the TRC's Final Report, released in 2016, characterized the origins and implementation of the residential school system in the context of Canadian settler colonialism:

> For over a century, the central goals of Canada's Aboriginal policy were to eliminate Aboriginal governments, ignore Aboriginal rights, terminate the Treaties, and through a process of assimilation, cause Aboriginal peoples to cease to exist as distinct legal, social, cultural, religious, and racial entities in Canada. The establishment and operation of residential schools were a central element of this policy, which can best be described as "cultural genocide."[15]

It's worth pausing here for a moment to think about that terrible word—*genocide*—which we have already used in this chapter without commentary. Words have power, and the words we choose to narrate our personal and collective histories are deeply consequential. The word *genocide* is shocking, one which many Canadians and Americans generally wish to associate with other tyrannical regimes and countries, such as Nazi Germany, not good, peace-loving, benevolent, liberal democracies such as ours. To apply such a term to our past is to challenge the common perception of our national identities and disrupt the cherished, comforting, national myths, and origin stories we tell ourselves. It is thus perhaps understandable that many settler Canadians, even many of those who genuinely wish for reconciliation, have recoiled against the use of this term to describe Canada's historical relations with Indigenous peoples. But as novelist Thomas King puts it, "A great many compassionate people have called residential schools a national tragedy. And they were."[16] However, he goes on to point out that the term *tragedy* is disingenuous, since it implies that the devastating consequences of residential schools were somehow accidental and unintended and undesired, not the result of deliberate national and church policy. Moreover, it also puts into question the work of many settler missionaries and teachers who were motivated by "good intentions." The point, however, is that at root the purpose of the schools was to destroy peoples and

---

15. *Final Report of the Truth*, 1. Hereafter cited as TRC Report.
16. King, *Inconvenient Indian*, 120.

cultures. To call an event a national tragedy or to call it genocide is to place that event in a different story. And hard as it is to hear, it is our assumption in what follows that the word *genocide* is the truthful one.

So what were the residential schools, and where did they come from? In many ways the story of Canada's history of cultural genocide as enacted in the residential school system is continuous with the long history of relations between European colonists and Indigenous peoples in the Americas since the encounter occurred after 1492. That momentous, world-changing encounter brought into contact peoples and cultures from the so-called Old and New Worlds for the first time. While these encounters were incredibly diverse and varied, settler Europeans over time came to share a common set of assumptions about Indigenous peoples that were—and remain—foundationally and destructively durable. First, they assumed that Indigenous peoples were uncivilized, possibly inhuman savages in dire need of Christianization and civilization. This "myth of the savage," as Canadian historian Olive Dickason called it, was a narrative projection that prevented Europeans from seeing the astonishing complexity and vitality of Indigenous cultures, politics, social structures, legal systems, and religions, and it became the frame through which the settler colonialism of Europeans justified five centuries of assimilationist and genocidal policies.[17] Second, a complementary set of attitudes coalesced in an ideology of conquest collectively known as the "Doctrine of Discovery." Europeans came to assume that the New World was empty or unused or unoccupied land—*terra nullius*—and this provided the legal, moral, philosophical, and religious legitimation for colonizing the New World. This ideology was a kind of legal magic that rendered invisible (to settlers) the Indigenous sovereignties and cultures as being inherently illegitimate. These two concepts—the myth of the savage and the Doctrine of Discovery—remain central to continuing patterns of settler colonialism today. If genuine reconciliation is to occur, quite frankly, settler Canadians and Americans will need to repudiate these false narratives completely. More broadly, these narratives are foundational to the national origin myths of Canada and the United States; disrupting these stories is thus deeply unsettling because our origin myths are comforting and normalizing.

These narratives, long-lasting and duplicitous as they were, continued to be foundational when Canada became a nation-state in 1867 and

---

17. See Dickason, *Myth of the Savage*.

began to enact colonial policies regarding Indigenous peoples, especially in the West, which settler Canadians wished to colonize and which was crucial to the vision of white politicians for a continental nation. Through treaties, and through paternalistic and colonial pieces of legislation like the Indian Act (1876), Canada sought to regulate, expropriate, and assimilate Indigenous peoples. As the TRC Final Report puts it, "Aboriginal people were expected to have ceased to exist as a distinct people with their own governments, cultures, and identities."[18]

A key element of these plans was education, especially education for Indigenous children. If Indigenous people were to disappear, their children would have to be educated in Western ways. And if they were to be civilized and Christianized, Indigenous spirituality, cultural traditions, and languages would have to be eradicated. Early on, federal officials argued that the state should fund the schools but they should be run and operated by churches. And they were, many of them, for over a century by the Catholic, United, Presbyterian, and Anglican churches in Canada. This collusion between church and state in the civilizational task of colonialism paradoxically harnessed the missionary zeal of white Christians to the task of subverting and eliminating Indigenous cultures. Since children were seen as particularly important for the task of cultural conversion and assimilation, government and church-run residential schools were established, because children could be more effectively trained if they were removed from the cultural influence of their parents and communities. Many were forcibly removed from their families and sent to live at great distances away from home in deeply alienating, abusive, and exploitative contexts.

The famous photo below depicts the ideal before-and-after vision of the residential schools—if viewed from the vantage point of those who created and ran the schools. In the first image, a young Indigenous residential student arrives at the school wearing the traditional clothing of his people; in the second, the same boy, now clad in settler clothing, is "civilized."

---

18. TRC Report, 53.

Re-Forming History

FIGURE 9

The schools operated for over a century and the last residential school in Canada closed in 1996, but not before enormous damage had been done to generations of Indigenous children. Further, the residential schools left painful legacies of intergenerational trauma, including the loss of cultures, languages, and cosmologies.

The TRC itself was created as part of a settlement to the largest class-action lawsuit in Canadian history. It was Indigenous peoples themselves who began to speak of their experiences. It was not, in the end, white settler Christians who brought this crime to the nation's attention, nor was it the federal government. Power and injustice are almost never challenged by those who wield or benefit from it, and it must be clear that the animating resistance to the practices of cultural genocide came from the extraordinary resilience of Indigenous peoples who have never been quiescent in the face of Western colonialism. On very few occasions did settler Canadians raise objections to the policies of residential schools. In the 1980s and 1990s a number of Christian denominations—the United Church, the Presbyterian Church of Canada, and the Anglican Church, all of which directly operated residential schools on behalf of the federal government—started to hear the ongoing voices of residential school survivors and began to initiate processes of apology and reconciliation for their complicity in colonialism and genocide. At the same time, survivors themselves began to sue the churches and the federal government for the abuse and suffering they had experienced in the schools. These lawsuits (which are still ongoing) grew in number and coalesced into major class-action proceedings, the largest of which resulted in a negotiated settlement with the federal government and the major churches. This agreement, signed in 2006, is the Indian Residential Schools Settlement Agreement (IRSSA), and it contained a number of components: an expansive program of financial compensation for survivors, support for Indigenous health initiatives, a pledge to create programs to commemorate the residential schools across the country, and the creation of the TRC itself. Stephen Harper's public apology on behalf of Canadians, heartfelt as it may have been, was not strictly speaking a voluntary act; it was a condition of the lawsuit settlement.

The TRC conducted its work from 2008–2015, when it issued its final report. The range of its activities was wide-ranging and extensive. As a history-making process, the TRC's reach was astonishing. The TRC took and will preserve testimony and statements from over 6,000 people, created a massive archives (in spite of the obstruction of the federal government) of documents and other historical materials that related to the residential schools, and established the National Centre for Truth and Reconciliation at the University of Manitoba. The archives are shaped by the conviction that "preserving the records is about much more than holding documents in a vault. By incorporating Indigenous perspectives on memory, archival practice and ownership, we are creating something new—a decolonizing archive built on principles of respect, honesty, wisdom, courage, humility, love and truth." Further, "the truth contained within the records housed at the NCTR will fuel new research, understanding, learning and reconciliation for years to come and will play an essential role in healing as we move forward as a nation."[19]

In addition, the TRC was charged with funding truth and reconciliation events at the local level, and to recommend commemorative activities so these stories will not be forgotten. Its largest public activities were held at seven national events, including the one in Edmonton we attended in March 2014. These four-day events included education and cultural performances, and opportunities for settler Canadians to make public gestures of reconciliation, as our university did. But at the core of all of these events

---

19. National Centre for Truth and Reconciliation, "Archives at the NTCR," paras. 1 and 2. See the full NCTR Archives statement here: http://nctr.ca/archives.php.

were the voices and stories of the survivors themselves. Statements by survivors were gathered in public Sharing Panels or Sharing Circles, or in cases where the testimony was too raw or personal, through private conversations with statement gatherers. Health and psychological support workers were always present for those who spoke and for those who listened.[20] In a subversive way, the TRC events brought those who were at the margins into the center, thus inverting the triumphalistic settler myth of Canadian nationalism. They asked those of us who are settlers to listen, to be silent, to be converted by stories of pain and loss and suffering, but also of great courage and recovery and resilience. We will not repeat any of the stories we heard. They are not our stories—they do not belong to us, and they are not ours to share.

No Reconciliation Without Truth

How might non-Indigenous Christian historians respond to the TRC? If these apologies are to be truly incarnated, they must be accompanied by transformed social relationships and by new narratives about Canada's ecclesial and national history. "Ecclesial repentance undermines itself if the suffering of those whom the church has harmed is rendered invisible," says theologian Jeremy Bergen.[21] We would suggest that something of what Johann Baptist Metz is saying is evident in the work of the TRC—this is dangerous memory, a kind of antihistory whose postcolonial critique threatens the content and meaning of our accepted national myths, such as our progressive multiculturalism and the doctrine of discovery, for example. Whether or not Canada will listen to the TRC is another question, of course. As we mentioned at the beginning of this chapter, Prime Minister Stephen Harper offered the apology on behalf of Canadians for the Indian Residential Schools, but then stated in a speech on September 26, 2011, that Canada has no history of colonialism. Settler Canadians may have a way to go in revisualizing their colonial past if this example of willful forgetfulness is any indication.

If we look at the TRC as a model for wholeheartedly Christian practices and liturgies for history, two themes come to mind.

First, the deliberate framing and permeation of all the TRC events—small and large—with worship, ritual, and ceremony in a way that liturgically

20. TRC Report, 26.
21. Bergen, *Ecclesial Repentances*, 12.

joined together survivors and perpetrators, witnesses and observers, creatures and Creator, people and land. Indigenous sacred ceremonies, which had been hidden away and suppressed by the structures of Western colonialism, were placed at the heart of the TRC's work. These ceremonies and traditions were linked to the work of right remembering, to the resurgent healing of Indigenous peoples whose cultures and bodies had been so long disrespected, and to the worshipful commitment to repentance from those in many Christian traditions who joined them in humility and conviction that the future might look different. The TRC intentionally placed ceremony at the center of all the events to establish the spiritual and ethical framework for the proceedings. Elders and Traditional Knowledge Keepers offered prayers and teachings. Smudges, pipe ceremonies, and other rituals occurred regularly throughout. At each event, a sacred fire was lit and cared for by Elders and Fire Keepers. The fire was used for prayers and tobacco offerings, "as well as to receive the tissues from the many tears shed during each event." The ashes from each fire were saved and brought to the subsequent event, to be added to the next sacred fire and "thus gathering in sacred memory the tears of an entire country."[22] We can attest personally to the generous and spacious hospitality that these rituals gave the people of all faiths as they wrestled from various vantage points with the task of reconciliation. Many Christian churches and denominations across Canada, meanwhile, responded to the TRC with services and gestures of apology in which they pledged themselves to new relationships.

Second, the primacy of storytelling, listening, and bearing witness. There can be no reconciliation without truth, but on what basis do we acknowledge truth? Settler scholar Paulette Regan offers some very useful insights about how genuine reconciliation and decolonization requires a changed ethical and moral framework: "How do we honour principles of witnessing and criteria for making, legitimizing, and recording acts of restitution and apology that use story, ceremony, and symbolic ritual in scared spaces?"[23] Storytelling, listening, and witnessing are embedded in the cultural practices of many Indigenous peoples, but these terms have much different connotations in Western cultural practice. For the former, storytelling truth is essentially relational, whereas for the latter we tend to

---

22. These descriptions are based on our own observations of the TRC's National Event in Edmonton in March 2013, as well as the TRC Report, 270-71.

23. Regan, *Unsettling the Settler Within*, 192.

judge "truth" by external or legal measurements of objectivity. But as Regan asks:

> How do settlers bear witness? That is, how do we listen and respond authentically and ethically to testimonies—stories of colonial violence, not with colonial empathy but as a testimonial practice of shared truth telling that requires us to be vulnerable, to question openly our accepted world views and cherished assumptions about our colonial history and identity? How do we learn to listen differently, taking on our responsibility to decolonize ourselves, making space for Indigenous history and experience? How do we move beyond denial and moral indifference toward acknowledging a history of violence? For settlers, the stories about residential schools are deeply *unsettling*. They are filled with experiences that overturn our cultural identity as a nation of peacemakers. They chronicle violence and dispossession that we do not want to hear, because they shake us to the core. But they are also potentially transformative.[24]

We hope the Metzian echoes of dangerous memory are evident in those questions, in the ways in which the TRC invited settlers to listen differently, to not impose our own voices, to be silent, to welcome the opportunity for transformative conversion, to feel. Storytelling and truth-telling are embedded in relationships, and some stories are not ours to tell. *How* we bear witness matters. To listen poorly is to do harm. To listen and to bear witness is to open ourselves to the unsettling, uncomfortable task of justice and reconciliation.

This point on bearing witness requires more elaboration, because some have criticized the TRC for this emphasis. Some observers and scholars have been rather critical of the "history-doing" or "history-making" capacity of the TRC. Whatever good the TRC did (or what TRCs do in general), the accusation from some is that they don't do good history. They criticize what they see as the public performance of the survivor's testimony, the liturgies that generate certain accepted reactions and identities while discounting others, and the potential for retraumatization for those witnesses who testify about the brutalization and violence they experienced. The TRC, according to some critics, had as much capacity to create indignation and new hostilities as it did truth and reconciliation. Such is the argument of Ronald Niezen, for example, who spent years as a very careful observer of the TRC in Canada, and who has criticized the history-making process

---

24. Regan, *Unsettling the Settler Within*, 190–91.

that the TRC's rituals created. In part, he says, the TRC created publics that "are persuaded more by emotion than by the historian's sense of complex interconnections or the reason of dispassionate justice."[25] Certainly people may be drawn into deeper connection with the issues by their curiosity and compassion. But he argues, "Seeking historical truth in conditions in which testimony often has heightened qualities of public performance, or in which approval is garnered for emotional poignancy, moral clarity, and narrative continuity, is inimical to 'historical truth.'" And again, he says, "The goal of expressing affirmation toward survivors is fundamentally at odds with cultivating a historical truth to serve as a foundation for a new narrative of the state."[26]

This last point is particularly problematic, although Niezen's critique is valid to the extent that it evinces a concern for the spiritual and psychological health of survivors who testified. The possibilities for re-traumatization as individuals told their stories are profound, but in fact the TRC did an exceptional job establishing protocols and supports for protecting the health of those who testified. What is objectionable, we argue, are his essential assumptions about reconciliation, historical truth-telling, and who they are for. In addition, we question the assumption that performative and emotional testimony is somehow unreliable and that it provides an insufficient foundation for public justice and reconciliation for the nation-state. Western historical practices, as we have argued, certainly privileges the rational, the dispassionate, the objective, and the critical engagement with the facts. The emotional layer (for lack of a better term), we are trained to assume, is what we have to dig beneath or brush away to get at the truth of what really happened or what the past means—especially so if we are to base our forward walk to reconciliation on such narratives. But to distrust and dismiss the emotional testimonies of Indigenous survivors is to negate their truth and to assess them via colonial Western practices, thus preserving the colonial structures and ideologies that provided the frame and justification for cultural genocide in the first place. And this critique passes over questions of power and authority: *Who* gets to determine whether testimony is true or rational—historians or those who testify? This assumption deliberately places the (settler) historian's truth (and historians themselves) somehow outside the narrative as judging outsiders and arbiters rather than as active witnesses, which are not the same thing.

25. Niezen, *Truth and Indignation*, 147–48.
26. Niezen, *Truth and Indignation*, 150.

Reconciliation, Decolonization, and Historical Practices: The Problem of Method

When it comes to reconciliation, furthermore, there is much more to consider than just the sins of the past, or how we think about history. We also need to reconsider how we as Christian academic historians do history—our methods and practices.

To make this case, let us take you to a place you might not expect: to the Arctic, and with a recent Canadian discovery of such importance that it warranted the personal participation of our former prime minister, Stephen Harper. In September 2014, high in the frozen North, Harper beamed as he stood in front of television cameras and announced what he called a "truly historic moment for Canada." The discovery? Nothing less than one of the ships from the ill-fated Franklin Expedition, which had disappeared in the 1840s into the Arctic ice and into Canadian legend (with the loss of over 150 men) in a failed search for the Northwest Passage. The fate of the expedition, one rehearsed frequently in Canadian fiction and song, had remained a mystery for almost 170 years. Dozens of searches had been mounted in the years since to find the ships and to find survivors, and when hope dwindled, their remains. When the wreckage of one of the ships was finally found by the Canadian scientific team, Ryan Harris, one of the lead archaeologists on the expedition, said—in that ultimate of Canadian superlatives—that finding the ship was "like winning the Stanley Cup." In his official announcement, Harper declared that "Franklin's ships are an important part of Canadian history given that his expeditions, which took place nearly 200 years ago, laid the foundations of Canada's Arctic sovereignty."[27] It's a strange thing, really. How an expedition under British authority that ended in catastrophe and rumors of cannibalism long before Canada was founded as a nation-state became the public-memory linchpin of Harper's nationalism is itself an interesting story, though one we will not explore here. Also strange to our ears was the phrase with which Harper concluded his press conference. God bless Canada, he said. We won't dwell on this, either, except to say that we Canadians are perhaps less used to such patriotic benedictions than Americans might be.

What was interesting to us (and many other observers) about this announcement and this "discovery" was who Harper thanked and didn't thank. In his remarks Harper acknowledged the historians, archaeologists,

---

27. Woolf, "Canada Uses Franklin Expedition Wreck," paras. 10 and 12.

and scientists who, after great effort and expense, had solved the mystery. What he didn't acknowledge (a fact again much noted by others) is that the key to the location of the wreck, even the most accurate guide that was discounted until recently as unreliable, was Inuit oral tradition. The fact is, the Inuit knew where the wreck was all along, and had known since the expedition met its catastrophe—but no white Canadians would listen.

Our point for the moment is not to mount a wholesale postcolonial critique against Western systems of historical knowledge, nor is it to romanticize traditional oral memory as somehow inherently better than Western historical methods; but it is useful to call attention to both as embedded in certain kinds of practices. Consider the remarkable achievement and gift it was to harbor this story in unbroken oral communal memory, the practices by which the story was preserved by the local Inuit over 170 years. "Something important happened here," we might imagine them saying to one another. "No one may ever believe us, but we must remember this." Consider the strength of that impulse, how profoundly such memory is embedded in embodied relationships, but also its fragility and seeming impermanence, how easily the thread of memory might have been snapped. It's important to remember not to view these practices as somehow being exotic, of course, a stance that still defines Indigenous traditional knowledge as other than the Western norm. We professional historians trained in Western intellectual practices like to think our knowledge of the past rests on firmer stuff, like archives and primary sources and texts. Indeed, as we have emphasized in this book, our professional scholarly practices—the ones which we teach our students in our Western schools, colleges, and universities—are predicated on such modernist and positivist assumptions about the relationship between evidence and conclusion, between data and facts. Could it be that colonialism itself is encoded in our practices? If so, and if we are serious about justice and reconciliation, how do we re-form our practices?

This irony, that in this case traditional Inuit memory trumped the codes and best practices of Western scientific and historical knowledge, has since generated much animated commentary. We should resist the temptation simply to find this story amusing, to read it merely as an innocuous example of the blindness of Western researchers who were guilty merely of some kind of oversight. This story fits into the wider pattern by which Western ways of knowing the world and history have been weaponized to do violence and injustice. In the twentieth century to the present, postcolonial theorists from Franz Fanon to Edward Said to Gayatri Spivak to Homi K. Bhabha, among many others, have identified the ways in which history and other disciplines have been deeply implicated in the silencing of non-Western traditions in the process of imperialism. In other words, the histories we tell in nation-states like Canada and the United States have been created in part as acts of willful forgetfulness that deliberately erase other narratives in the service of colonial sovereignty. The Doctrine of Discovery is just one example. And our historical methods—the liturgies that shape how we do history—have been put to the same purpose. The anecdote about the "discovery" of the Franklin expedition is part of the wider pattern of past and continuing colonial violence.

The term *epistemic injustice* is useful here, as it comprises not just what we know about the past (the "content" or the "story") but also how we know it (our methodologies). "Western knowledge systems are typically built on a rationalist, secular epistemology" that are "seen as principled, fair, and neutral," says Rebecca Tsosie. In contrast, "Indigenous knowledge systems are often seen as deficient because they are perceived as faith-based 'religious systems.'"[28] Such histories and ways of knowing the past (encoded in such things as the Doctrine of Discovery) that legitimized imperialisms continue to affect the contemporary legal and policy rights of Indigenous peoples worldwide because colonial structures still ignore Indigenous values and practices. As Métis/Cree poet Marilyn Dumont wrote in response to the Franklin ship story: "My question is, if the Inuit stories recount the location of the Franklin ship and 'researchers discovered' this material evidence through the Inuit Traditional Knowledge, why aren't the Inuit perceived as practitioners of formal systems of knowledge? Why aren't the Inuit ascribed 'discoverers?'" And Michael Stewart commented: "It's a thick knot: dead colonial explorers attempting to discover land already discovered by the Inuit are 'discovered' by present-day explorers using methods already discovered by the Inuit. And throughout it all, land claims, title, knowledge systems, authority and presence are systematically denied and extinguished." More bluntly, Stewart wrote:

> You'd be tempted to call this systematic, centuries-old erasure a sociological phenomenon—one that is repeated and re-inscribed on all our social structures: a justice system that is deaf to Aboriginal stories, an electoral system that disenfranchises Aboriginal voices, an educational system that ignores or denigrates Aboriginal

---

28. See Tsosie, "Indigenous Peoples, Anthropology," 359.

knowledge and meaning making. A sociological iceberg so large that we can't even strike our boats against it because we're already inside.

We *could* call it a sociological phenomenon—but I'll just call it a crime.[29]

And he's right. It's interesting and eye-opening to consider this problem through the lens of Indigenous research methodologies. A fascinating and instructive set of perspectives on the relationship between colonial knowledge systems and Indigenous ways of knowing comes from *Decolonizing Methodologies: Research and Indigenous Peoples* by Linda Tuhiwai Smith, a Maori scholar from New Zealand. She starts with the observation that the term "research" itself is "probably one of the dirtiest words in the Indigenous world's vocabulary." Western colonial research practices were part of the tools of empire, part of the architecture through which imperialists justified and rationalized their conquest and exploitation of the Indigenous "Other." Thus, Smith says, "it galls us that Western researchers and intellectuals can assume to know all that it is possible to know of us, on the basis of their brief encounters with some of us." And it "angers us when [research] practices . . . are still employed to deny the validity of Indigenous peoples' claims to existence, to land and territories, to the right of self-determination, to the survival of our languages and forms of cultural knowledge, to our natural resources and systems for living within our environments."[30] Reclaiming Indigenous sovereignties and knowledge practices are profound acts of resistance at odds with the political tenets and research terminologies of the West. Where Western methodologies emphasize words like *neutrality* and *objectivity*, terms like *healing, decolonization, spiritual,* and *recovery* are key to what Smith calls the Indigenous research agenda that operates from the margins in the pursuit of social justice.[31] As Smith puts it, the writing and research of Indigenous peoples and allied anti-colonial scholars suggests that the way out of colonialism "exists within our own alternative, oppositional ways of knowing."[32] She notes the extensive connection between Christian missions and the attempt to obliterate Indigenous traditions, but locates the core of resistance in those traditions. "The arguments of different Indigenous peoples based on

---

29. Stewart, "Harper's Franklin 'Discovery,'" paras. 9–11.
30. Smith, *Decolonizing Methodologies*, 1.
31. Smith, *Decolonizing Methodologies*, 122.
32. Smith, *Decolonizing Methodologies*, 204.

spiritual relationships to the universe, to the landscape and to stones, rocks, insects, and other things, seen and unseen, have been difficult arguments for Western systems of knowledge to deal with or accept," she points out. "The values, attitudes, concepts and language embedded in beliefs about spirituality represent . . . the clearest contrast and mark of difference between Indigenous peoples and the West."[33]

Shaun Wilson offers another view of Indigenous research methods by asserting that "research is ceremony." He argues for a view of an Indigenous research paradigm that is based on two major premises: that "the shared aspect of an Indigenous ontology and epistemology is relationality (relationships do not merely shape reality, they *are* reality)," and that the "shared aspect of an Indigenous axiology and methodology is accountability to relationships."[34] To put it more simply, *knowledge* as such cannot exist outside of relationships—between people, between people and nature or the land, etc. Viewing research as ceremony implies, among other things, that "the purpose of any ceremony is to build stronger relationships or to bridge the distance between aspects of our cosmos and ourselves."[35] Wilson works to identify how Indigenous research is different from dominant system scholarship (in which we must honestly locate ourselves) from Western systems of research and knowledge that are instrumental, individualistic, and "rational." Instead it is based on relationships with people and with creation. And, he says, "If research doesn't change you as a person, then you haven't done it right."[36]

We find much that is life-giving in these ideas and practices—the emphasis on faith, on relationships, on research which enacts change that is personal and communal, on justice, and on reclaiming the voices, histories, and practices of those who have been silenced. But we mustn't steal or appropriate Indigenous knowledge or methods—that also replicates colonial exploitation. And for all our good intentions, it is still an act of presumption—perhaps even an offensive one—to propose the task of "re-forming history" to the community of academic Christian historians and students when we ourselves are embedded in colonial and academic structures, hierarchies, and practices as white, middle-class, Christian, North American cisgendered males. "Physicians, heal yourselves," we can hear dissenting

---

33. Smith, *Decolonizing Methodologies*, 78.
34. Wilson, *Research is Ceremony*, 7.
35. Wilson, *Research is Ceremony*, 11.
36. Wilson, *Research is Ceremony*, 135.

voices say, and rightly so. We do not write this book from situations of risk or danger, professional or personal, and in fact the act of publishing this book in some fashion only deepens our entrenchment in our own privilege because publication is the currency of prestige (such as it is) in our profession. Publishing a book actually enhances our credentials and our authority and our power. If we apply Jesus's instruction to the young rich man—"sell all you own, and follow me" (Matt 19:21)—to our call in this book for a subversive, even radical reforming of Christian historical practices, then by our own standards we find ourselves lacking deeply. We are part of the problem. How then do we faithfully enact our vocation to be agents of reconciliation?

John Tosh, the author of a solid and perceptive text on the practices of history, *The Pursuit of History*, notes very simply that "Working historians for the most part shrink from the full implications of postcolonial theory."[37] Our working thesis for re-forming history is that Christian historians must not shrink from them. History practiced from a modernist colonial perspective often does the following: it explains why a colonizing power deserves to be in power; it silences and erases the voices (and histories) of the colonized; it rationalizes and normalizes why the colonized deserve to be ruled and subjugated; and it creates mythologies and liturgies and methodologies that defend colonial power and privilege as being natural or providential or divinely ordained colonial realities. The Western historical profession is founded on such verities. So, recalling the warning from John de Gruchy which we reviewed earlier in this chapter, and given the modernist, objectivist, colonial foundations of the historical profession, how do we embody practices of historical remembering in our discipline

- That are not hegemonic?
- That are not ethnocentric?
- That are not racist?
- That are not patriarchal?
- That are not paternalistic?
- That are not salvationist?
- That are not uncomplicated?
- That are not ahistorical?

---

37. Tosh, *Pursuit of History*, 250.

- That are not depoliticized?
- That are not hierarchical?
- That do not silence?
- That love our neighbors?

For all our limitations, the call of Micah 6:8 is still operative for Christian historians, as is the promise of Christian hope. And we cannot respond defensively or be paralyzed with guilt. What kinds of practices should Christian historians embody when trying to live out these commitments to apology, justice, and reconciliation? Again, the answers to this question must be situational, contextual, and specific, but here are a few examples.

1. From the TRC itself, there is a series of practical steps that settler Christian historians can apply to their vocation as teachers and scholars. In its Final Report the TRC issued 94 "Calls to Action," a broad-ranging set of commitments that are a preliminary blueprint to reconciliation between settler Canadians and Indigenous peoples. Many pertain directly to history, education, commemoration, and research. Some of these include the following:

    a. Honoring Indigenous spirituality in ways that recognize the extraordinary vitality of those traditions, that acknowledge Christian culpability for trying to eliminate them, and that sees these traditions as sources of healing and self-determination for Indigenous peoples;[38]
    b. Rewriting history curriculum and educational materials to remedy the gaps in historical understanding that continue to render Indigenous people as invisible or supplanted;[39]
    c. Transforming the education system into one that treats Indigenous and Euro-Canadian or Western knowledge systems with equal space and respect;[40]
    d. In partnership with Indigenous researchers, whose cultural, political, and spiritual traditions have great resources on these questions, conducting research on the reconciliation process, which "can inform how Canadian society can mitigate intercultural conflicts, strengthen civic trust, and build social

---

38. TRC Report, 224.
39. TRC Report, 235.
40. TRC Report, 239.

capacity and practical skills for long-term reconciliation";[41]
  e. Working to reshape and re-story Canada's archives and national museums, institutions which have acted as part of the "architecture of imperialism" by silencing and rendering invisible Indigenous culture and history;[42]
  f. To work to repudiate the Doctrine of Discovery as a colonial artifact that continues to act to delegitimize Indigenous sovereignties and land rights.[43]

In other words, there are practical steps by which settler historians can decolonize their practices and contribute in their teaching and research to the work of reconciliation.

2. From historian Paulette Regan, whose ideas about listening and witnessing we have already considered, we get an "unsettling pedagogy of history and hope." She argues that settler Canadians "cannot just theorize about decolonizing and liberatory struggle: we must experience it, beginning with ourselves as individuals, and then as morally and ethically responsible socio-political actors in society."[44] Particularly important in this process is the capacity for individuals in the majority culture to recognize their own complicity in colonialism, to not ignore the ways in which power and privilege shelter them from the unsettling counternarratives the TRC and other Indigenous voices profess about Canada's (and America's) history. We who are settlers should be discomforted by the colonial narratives and practices that have silenced and harmed. Regan conceptualizes history, then, not simply as the study of the past ("the facts and interpretations through which we gain knowledge about our social world") but as a critical learning practice, a pedagogy that disrupts and dislodges us from our comfort zones, "an experiential strategy that invites us to learn how to listen differently to the testimonies of Indigenous people."[45] If settler Canadians fail to move beyond either denial or guilt, we will not be capable of genuine reconciliation and transformation. Indeed, she says, "Reconciliation is not a goal but a place of transformative

---

41. TRC Report, 242.
42. TRC Report, 246.
43. TRC Report, 191.
44. Regan, *Unsettling the Settler Within*, 23–24.
45. Regan, *Unsettling the Settler Within*, 50.

encounter where all participants gather the courage to face our troubled history without minimizing the damage that has been done, even as we learn new decolonizing ways of working together that shift power and perceptions."[46] Reconciliation and justice require action, in other words, and those of us who have benefited from colonialism cannot imagine that a commitment to change won't cost us something—power, space, privilege.

3. Lastly, from Mennonite theologian W. Derek Suderman, we get a meditation on Jubilee, occasioned by the purchase of his family home in Waterloo, Ontario, Canada. The land on which he lives (and on which all North Americans live) is unceded, stolen land. In this case, his home is on land that was taken by white settlers in what was called the Haldimand Tract in the 1780s. Suderman began to think about his presence and ownership of the land in connection with the Old Testament principle of Jubilee, the revolutionary Israelite injunction (see Leviticus 25) that every fifty years all land should be returned to its original owners. Suderman became convicted by "an uncomfortable question: How do I follow the one whose Gospel proclaimed a Jubilee orientation and embodied a way of being that challenged the empire of his day?"[47] He goes on to suggest how settler Christians might work to support Indigenous vindication on land claims and treaty rights rooted in historical practices of colonial dispossession. By analogy, Christian settler historians might work for Jubilee history, to re-story the land by challenging "our tendency to monopolize the role of speaker in history."[48] We need new stories, we need to listen—not speak—and we need to cede back the territory we have claimed which is not ours.

The call to Jubilee as a model of reconciliation is indeed a radical one, a call to conversion and justice. The Old Testament theologian Walter Brueggemann understands the practice of Jubilee as a collective discipline of holiness, "so that holiness becomes a practice of neighborly justice."[49] It's an apt metaphor for how Canada might consider its colonial history and commitment to reconciliation. And it is an appropriate image through

---

46. Regan, *Unsettling the Settler Within*, 211.
47. Suderman, "Reflections of a Christian Settler," 269.
48. Suderman, "Reflections of a Christian Settler," 271.
49. Brueggemann, *Introduction to the Old Testament*, 73.

which Christian historians might reframe their work and practices. It will be extraordinarily difficult work, and it will take time. For some of us it will be unsettling and uncomfortable, even fearful, as we examine our prejudices and complicity, as our unearned privileges are shaken. Justice Murray Sinclair, the chair of the TRC, often said that it took seven generations to create the catastrophe that was the residential schools, and it will take seven generations to heal and reconcile from it. We pray it will not take so long, but we insist that if the TRC's goals are to be realized, they must be accompanied by transformed social relationships and liturgies, and by new narratives and methodologies about Canada's church and national history. If we are honest about our commitment to decolonization and reconciliation, that will have to be manifested visibly in our academic institutions, our pedagogies, and our research methodologies. If we are truly serious about doing history that heals, Christian historians need to be part of that Jubilee vocation.

CONCLUSION
Endings, But Not an End

This book is ending, perhaps to your great relief. But this is also a beginning, for as we know there is no end to history, just endings.[1] We have been arguing for the need to re-form history, to reconsider the practices and liturgies that shape and constrain how we do history. We have been arguing that it is crucial that we move beyond modernity in our work as Christian historians and transcend the limitations imposed by history as a professional discipline. History was shaped by the intellectual imperatives of modernity, by the constraints of institutionalization and professionalization, and by the influence of industrial methods of producing knowledge. The modernist approach to history has generated a series of practices that are in need of renewal. There is no road map, of course. We will make the path by walking, and we will make the path together. History as a discipline has always developed by striking outward in search of the new and looking inward to renew. The starting point for our journey in this book was the 95 theses, and we invite you to return to them, to read this ending as a kind of beginning. We hope they cause you to pause or question or reflect: they may provoke or irritate, bore, or annoy you, but we hope that they prepare you to think about doing history differently.

Before we leave the beaten track we offer four propositions for you to ponder as you consider for yourself what doing history Christianly might look like. These four propositions are not neat and distinct; they are interwoven, each reinforcing and supporting one another. Cumulatively, they echo the themes we've raised and the questions we've asked in this book, and they suggest pathways for re-formed Christian historical practices. We will address each in turn:

1. Steedman, *Dust*, 142–54.

Conclusion

Proposition 1: Historians should *ask themselves*, "Who is my neighbor?"

Perhaps the place to start for historians is to restore the basic calling of all Christians—to love God with all their heart and mind and soul and strength, and to love their neighbors as themselves—to the center of their work. As you probably know, this question was posed to Jesus in Luke 10 by an expert in the law trying to test Jesus. Jesus answered by telling the parable of the Good Samaritan. In it he outlined how the Samaritan—the traveler who stopped his journey, crossed over the various cultural and other taboos to assist the wounded man—proved to be the neighbor to the man, as he was the "one who showed mercy." Maybe this parable has something to teach us about the role of the historian and their dealings with the people of the past. We think that the idea of "historian as Good Samaritan" expresses a few key ideas.

One, the imperative is love and care. When the Samaritan stumbles across the man who has been robbed, his first instinct is not to try and work out what happened. He doesn't treat it like a criminal investigation, trying to establish the chain of events, causes, motive, and so on. He doesn't treat it like a mystery to be figured out. He doesn't use it as a stick to beat the authorities with for failing to protect people. He doesn't despair at the levels of crime and violence in society. No, he crosses over and tends to the wounded man. The Good Samaritan story talks of the moral stance of the historian toward the people of the past. The Good Samaritan interrupted his journey, tended to the man, took time to ensure he was looked after, and used his own resources to provide welfare. When he saw him, he had compassion. We might also say that his first impulse was to listen, to bear witness, and it may be that our responsibilities as Christian historians may be to stop there—to listen only, and not to tell stories that are not ours. His actions were not driven by curiosity, a desire for knowledge, but by an attitude of mercy and care. The bigger issues—about crime or justice or restitution—can be dealt with later. Our first instinct should be love and care.

In the same way, we believe that the historian should overwhelmingly tend to the past (and the people therein) with love, care, mercy, and compassion. This was the essence of Jesus's teaching. Mercy manifested itself in specific actions. And the Christian historian should seek to display the same qualities when they go about their work. The compulsion for knowledge and to use that knowledge for our own ends must be resisted in favor of an ethic of love. Mercy should extend not merely to how we do our work, but also to the people whom we study. Our vocation as Christian historians is to hold the people of the past lovingly in our hands, and take seriously the God-given responsibility to tend to them lovingly and truthfully. Our work should be infused with love, mercy, and compassion. It also helps us to consider that perhaps the most fruitful and beneficial way to study the past is not as the detached observer, but incarnationally, walking alongside, caring.

Two, the story of the Good Samaritan should teach us not to forget the marginalized, rejected, downtrodden, and wounded in the past. It's very easy when we enter the past, to get caught up with the famous, the powerful, the winners, the great and the good, the popular, to be drawn to the sensational, to controversy, conspiracy, and infamy. Yet if the Good Samaritan story teaches us anything, it's that we have to choose not to walk past the ordinary, not to pass by on the other side. History, because it is the story of human beings, is replete with the wounded, the injured, the missing, the silent and the dead. The past is full of people we know nothing about. The past is full of those who have fallen prey to the schemes of others: victims of failed utopias, victims of the abuses of power, victims of warfare, famine, and genocide. We think we have a responsibility to remember them, to include them in our writings, not just to dismiss them with a wave of our pens. We have to stop and tell their stories. Our concern should be to treat them as people in their own right, dignify them, and give them a voice. Proverbs 31:8, for example, talks about the responsibility to "open your mouths for the mute, for the rights of all who are destitute."

Three, we should consider carefully the cultural taboos the Good Samaritan had to confront. This has echoes in Jesus's command to love our enemies. We need to cross over and love our enemies too. This is a very difficult one. We are called to love both justice and mercy. Maybe we need to find a way to tell a rounded, holistic, humanized story of their lives, to extend grace to them in the same way that God has extended grace to us. Understanding human lives in all their complexity, their flaws as well as their qualities, is an important part of the task of the Christian historian. We should always flee from making hasty judgments, simplistic pronouncements, and generalizations. For example, one of the most awful episodes in twentieth-century history was the Rape of Nanking. Unspeakable atrocities were carried out against the local Chinese population by the occupying Japanese soldiers. One of the shockingly paradoxical parts of this story is that one of the "heroes" who acted to save thousands of lives was John

Conclusion

Rabe, a German engineer and a member of the Nazi party. A Nazi *saving* lives? It seems implausible. But we would do well to remember that those whom we might vilify for their actions bleed like you and me when they are cut. Studying the past means being prepared to be confronted with things that might force you to rethink your view of the world.

Four, we should resist the siren songs of curiosity. For in curiosity there lies the road to the aspiration to know all, and to master all through our knowledge. Although the desire to seek understanding—to know in whole, not in part, to know the beginning and the end, to know the big picture—is natural and can be good and profitable, we must be wary of it too. And so there is a strong imperative for Christians to make sure we don't miss the "particular, the limited, the specific,"[2] when we are striving for something bigger. For this was the way of the Good Samaritan. He was not trying to care for all the wounded, or trying to understand all the reasons for suffering and pain. No, he tended to the pain and hurt right in front of him, with all of his resources and care and attention. It's a recognition of our limits too. We can't do everything. But we can do something, and we can do it with love.

Five, the story of the historian as Good Samaritan points to the relationship between the narrator and their audience. The Good Samaritan story was told by Jesus in part *to shock* his audience, but also *to remind them to do likewise*. It is a story which confounds the audience, turning their preconceptions upside down and making them uncomfortable. It is also a story full of suffering *and* hope. It is complex and perplexing. We should think carefully about the importance of doing history that *serves life*. We should write our stories of the past not just to give a voice to those who have been silenced, but also to converse with those in our world today. By uncovering the hope in the past, we communicate hope to those who read our work in the present. By narrating stories of suffering, we remember those who have been marginalized and oppressed. We contemplate how we might mediate the people in the past—their lives, loves, and loss—to the people in the present. Our neighbors are not just those in the past, but those for whom we work in the present.

The point, then, is to think about our work as historians as *serving life* and *serving others*, not ourselves. It helps us to move away from the scramble of the career path, status, reputation, and rewards. Our motivation for studying the past is driven by an ethic of service, emphasizing our

---

2. Schweiger, "Seeing Things," 71.

responsibility to others: those in the past and those in the present. The Good Samaritan story reminds us of these responsibilities. We have to hold each other to account. When we seek to deny our public role, when we become too interested in status, career, rewards, and promotion, when we allow the past to be used by others for their own malevolent ends (political, ideological, religious, or commercial) we have denied our position and our responsibility. We need to be constantly holding each other in check. We need to reflect upon our methodological and ethical practices to ensure that we are doing what we should, in the way that we should. We need to reclaim a prophetic edge to our work: we should be irritants, dangerous, and subversive when necessary. We should be seeking truth and justice where there is none. We need to ensure that our work is serving others before anything else.

So, who is your neighbor?

Proposition 2: Historians should *see themselves* as living and working in a web of mutuality: they are to work *sans frontieres*, crossing borders of time and space, culture and belief.

In place of the triple alliance of modernist history—the aspiration for scientific objectivity, professionalism and heroic individualism—we desire an approach rooted in love, vocation, and mutuality. One of the many things we value about the study of the past is its ability to remind us of *our common shared humanity, and to connect us across time and space*. In other words: solidarity. We are talking here of the importance of *crossing over*, of having no boundaries or borders or barriers to divide us. As historians, we should work *sans frontieres*. We should see ourselves as threads in a single garment. As Martin Luther King Jr. put it so memorably in his letter from prison in Birmingham in August 1963,

> Moreover I am cognizant of the interrelatedness of all communities and states. I cannot sit idly by in Atlanta and not be concerned about what happens in Birmingham. Injustice anywhere is a threat to justice everywhere. We are caught in an inescapable network of mutuality, tied in a single garment of destiny. Whatever affects one directly affects all indirectly.[3]

So what does this mean?

3. King, "Letter from Birmingham Jail," 1.

Conclusion

We have to see ourselves differently, not as islands, not as separated from each other, not as independent. There are many borders or boundaries or divisions that exist to separate us. We have to cross these borders and live in this inescapable network of mutuality. You can probably think of the borders and barriers that exist in your context. For us, the following borders need to be crossed.

#Crosstheborder between Profession and Vocation

Our responsibilities in our work must extend way beyond the norms and standards of a professional organization. We are not a profession like carpenters, electricians, plumbers, or doctors, which require safeguards as to the quality of the work they produce. This does not mean that we ignore the conventions, methods, and practices that we should be using when we do our work. More on this below. We do need to assure people that we are working with integrity, and that we have robust safeguards which ensure the quality and validity of our work. But it must be much more than this. Our primary concern should not be with rules, regulations, conventions, and professional norms. Instead we need to practice our history through a hermeneutic of love. We affirm that knowledge should be practiced as love, not as power. The whole *ethos* around professionalism privileges the idea of knowledge as something to be possessed, accumulated, exchanged, and used for the benefit of the possessor. Professionalism exalts curiosity, which seems to be motivated by the need to possess as much knowledge as possible, as an end in itself. Professionalism creates a deep desire for control. Knowledge as love differs in almost all respects. It exalts kindness in dealing with the dead of the past. It seeks out wisdom. It listens to the voices of the people, attentive to them. It withholds judgment in favor of charity. We seek not our own good, but the good of others. Love delights in the simple presence of the other, lets them be who they are, and refuses to use them or control them. The imperative for the historian to cross the divide between profession and vocation lies in trying to meld together the imperative to work with integrity and diligence and the pursuit of excellence (implicit in the idea of the profession and being professional) with the idea—central to vocation—that this work is done in service of others. It is altruistic, other-regarding. It seeks not the fulfillment of the desires of the one called, but the ones to whom one is called to serve, be they students or readers or viewers. We need to resist the drift into professional specialization, narrow horizons, and disinterested detachment.

#Crosstheborder between the Academy and the Public Sphere

A growing tendency amongst professional historians has been to withdraw. Isolating themselves within their universities and their disciplinary communities and their specific research field, they have ceased interacting with the general public, or engaging with the world outside academia. They have, consequently, lost their public voice. Turning inward they have focused on the narrow demands of teaching and research, building their research profile, pursuing research grants and tenure, and generally eking out a career. But the human knowledge we call "history" is too important, too valuable, too significant to be left languishing in corridors and seminar rooms and obscure journals. History is used, abused, controlled, manipulated, and portrayed in all sorts of ways—good and bad, delightfully and terribly—by politicians, filmmakers, novelists, cartoonists, bloggers, and tour companies. And historians just watch, silent. Historians need to recover a sense of public purpose for their work and their activity which takes them out into the public spaces—real and virtual—in order to engage with the key debates and issues of our day. They should be informing debates around public policy. Providing context on decisions around foreign policy. Working with filmmakers regarding how the past is portrayed on film. Engaging with local and national authorities concerning what and how our communities should be remembering in our public spaces. Collaborating with museums and archives to make the past more accessible. Writing in newspapers and magazines and using social media to communicate with diverse audiences. The inescapably social and public role of the historian is to help people remember, to stop people forgetting, to speak truth to power, to reveal that which has been hidden, to comfort and to console and to disturb. We should be concerned about advocating for justice, both then and now. We should be concerned about speaking the truth. We should be concerned—wherever we live—with engaging the public in the critical debates and issues that face each society. We should be bringing diverse voices and perspectives into long-forgotten or neglected issues. We should be creating interest in the uses of the past in our public spaces. We should be starting conversations around the content of the history curricula in our schools. We care about the world we live in, and are engaged with it.

Conclusion

History should not be a private conversation within the academy. The past is too important to too many people.

#Crosstheborder of Time and Space

The relational dimension of the study of the past means that we have responsibilities to those who have gone before us, those we live with, and those who will come after us. Historians, we believe, have a significant responsibility to *build human solidarity* across time and space. We seek to bring to life those in the past who have been forgotten, silenced, marginalized, ignored, and oppressed. In so doing, we connect them with people in the present, and try to ensure their lives—however short or tragic—are remembered. For if we do not do this, who will? Who will remember the dead? Ensure their dignity? Our reach across time has to be complemented by a reach across space, and our responsibility to produce history which does two things simultaneously. One, it reaches across to overcome our differences and communicate the importance of our common humanity. This is not a case of denying or downplaying our differences, tensions, fissures, and conflicts as humans, but it does challenge the idea that the things that divide us are more important or more significant than the things we share.[4] Increasing globalization, the enduring power of nationalism, and controversies around migration and immigration make it vital that we as historians tell stories about the universality of the human experience. We need to do work on the things that unite us, not just those that divide. We need to counter the fragmentary tendencies inherent in identity history and politics, and balance that with stories of who we are as a species, irrespective of our color, ethnicity, beliefs, class, gender, or sexuality. This does not mean at all that we abandon research in these areas, but that we balance them with historians who research these common human experiences.

It also reaches out to recognize historic and systemic injustices done to particular groups of humans. Part of the call to human solidarity is to recognize those people groups—historically and contemporaneously—who have suffered exploitation, marginalization, oppression, and injustice. Recognizing these injustices also means working toward their eradication so that they might experience the dignity and equality which all humans need. Our web of mutuality must compel us to say that when one suffers

---

4. See, for example, the stimulating book by David Cannadine, *Undivided Past*.

we all suffer: "Whatever affects one directly affects all indirectly."[5] Solidarity calls us to stand with those who might be forgotten, those who have been silenced, and those who have been denied dignity. A particularly pressing need in our current world is for a history which overcomes ethnocentrism and aspires to universalism.

Jorn Rusen has attempted to suggest a few key practices to help all historians overcome ethnocentrism and develop a new mode of universal history rooted in a concept of humankind.[6] He argues for the following things to overcome ethnocentrism:

- A recognition of the principle of equality between self and others and asserting the principle of the mutual recognition of differences.

- To enable people to recognize the value of others requires historians everywhere to integrate negative historical experiences into the master narrative of one's own group. This also requires historians to engage with issues of mourning, lament, and forgiveness as each society learns to deal with these negative moments.

- An approach to the past which emphasizes contingency, discontinuity, and rupture: the present is not the only possible outcome of the historical process. Nothing is inevitable. The present order of things—distributions of wealth and power—are neither inevitable nor inherent in a particular culture, religion, or ethnic group, but are historically contingent.

- The past should be approached upon a polycentric basis and from multiple perspectives, and we need to look for ways to mediate and synthesize these different perspectives.[7]

We would add that for Christians, these ideas and practices are only amplified when we remind ourselves that we believe all people—past, present, and future—are image-bearers of God, the faces of Christ. Can there be a more important project for Christian historians than to contribute to a world which is seeking earnestly to transcend destructive differences?

So, are you ready to cross over??

---

5. King, "Letter from Birmingham Jail," 1.
6. Rusen, "How to Overcome Ethnocentrism," 118–29.
7. Rusen, "How to Overcome Ethnocentrism," 125–27.

CONCLUSION

Proposition 3: Historians should *remind themselves* of their humanity and be sensitive to the rich human qualities that lie in the past: hope, lament, suffering, beauty, and truth.

Historians are human beings. History should operate as a reminder of our humanity, and of our responsibilities to other humans. This puts human relationships at the heart of what we do, how we do it, and why we do it. To recover the human essence of our work means considering above all else the people we find in the archives, the people we write for, and the people we work with. How we treat others should be uppermost in our thinking and working. Much of the writing about history talks about historians sharing two key things in common: an acceptance of the significance of the study of the past ("history for its own sake") and a commitment to a set of shared practices. We think that a better place to start is instead to consider how the study of the past should remind us of who we are, of our connections with others, and our responsibilities to others, both dead and alive.[8] To reduce history merely to a set of shared practices is to denude it of its great power and significance, and turn it into something technical, professional, and utilitarian. To emphasize the value of history as knowledge for its own sake is to retreat from the calling to use our scholarship as part of our calling to love and serve others. Instead we see something else in history, something deeper, more human. Our practices are important in that they help us to do it well, and do it with integrity. But we need to move well beyond thinking about our practices. In particular, the depth and richness of the human experience should be viewed in our work. It should be about pursuing beauty, truth, and justice. It should seek to stir us emotionally. To lament. Grieve. Celebrate. Commemorate. Pursue truth. Wonder. Mystery. All those intangible elements that make human relationships and life so unpredictable and indefinable. If the summit of our ambition is to ensure accuracy, even-handedness, and excessive detail, then we are doing a grave disservice to all the stories and lives that we hold in our hands. We have so much to talk about. Let's not get stuck in vain attempts to show that we are

---

8. There have been many things written about this. Some of the most interesting and significant include, Champion, "What are Historians for?," 167–88; Katerberg, "Person of the Historian," 76–81; a special issue of *Diogenes* 42 (1994); Gorman, "Historians and Their Duties," 103–17; Fisch, "*Sati* and the Task," 361–68; Spiegel, "Presidential Address," 1–15; Leuchtenburg, "Presidential Address," 1–18; McCarraher, "On a Certain Blindness," 54–60; and de Baets, "Declaration on the Responsibilities," 130–64.

right. Instead let's make our history something that reminds us of what it means to be human.

One of the dimensions of history to which we must attend is its ability—if we are willing—to allow our encounter with the dead of the past to change us or even convert us. The practice of history can work a little like a set of spiritual disciplines. We learn to love those who are different. We learn to embrace uncertainty and contingency. We learn to accept that which we will never know. We learn to be humble in the face of our limited ability to know. We learn to listen to a whole range of voices. We seek to love. We seek the good of others. For we know that the path to a history that loves goes through the formation of our own characters as loving, gracious, compassionate seekers of truth, justice, and kindness in our work and in our world. But this hermeneutic of love does not come without a cost. Humans love, play, create, and sing. They do noble things and mundane things, but also terrible things. History is littered with tragedy—violence, suffering, pain, trauma—and it takes its toll on the historian if you allow yourself to feel. Immerse. Experience. Listen to the voices. Shed a tear. Some things you just don't want to read again, hear again, see again, but you can't unread it, unsee it, or unhear it. It hurts. So you keep it to yourself. It's too dark, too grim, too painful to share or talk about. So it sits inside you. Studying the past will form us in particular ways, but it can be a costly and difficult thing to do. To do the work of a historian is to open yourself up to the full spectrum of human actions, behaviors, practices, and beliefs. It can be frustrating. It can be crushing. It can be uplifting. But it should always remind us of our own humanity.

Proposition 4: Historians should *commit themselves* to a code of ethics.

History has a set of core practices, and these practices need to be done well and with integrity. But history is also much more than a set of practices. So, why a code of ethics, and what might that look like? A set of common standards for historians to follow can help to create a shared acceptance of good practices which will allow us to eliminate basic errors and mistakes in our work. These may be benign in nature (i.e., they have no agenda or malevolent intent), but the consequence may be less benign if it leads to faulty interpretations or a distorted understanding. A code of some kind, which addresses the basic practices and conventions of the discipline, is a good

Conclusion

way to safeguard against human error or deliberate manipulation. More than that, however, a code of ethics signals our best intentions in answer to the questions we've been asking in this book: Who should our practices as historians serve, and how should our practices direct how we love?

A code of ethics is not an original idea, of course. One example is a recent "Code of Conduct" put together by Suzannah Lipscomb. She concludes with the injunction that, "Our professional integrity as historians relies on our adherence to standards such as these."[9] More formally, the American Historical Association has set out a highly crafted "Statement on Standards of Professional Conduct."[10] In this twenty-page document, they set out the shared values of all practicing professional historians, and outlined some of the key conventions and approaches that historians should subscribe to if they are to maintain the highest standards of professionalism and integrity in their work. In essence this statement is the expression of a professional body seeking to ensure that it enjoys the trust and good faith of the people around it: students, journalists, scholars, organizations, journalists, and the general public.

These are worth a thorough look, and we encourage you to do so and compare these statements to the code of ethics we offer below because we wish to go a little further. If we might borrow from the Bolshevik Party's revolutionary program for a minute, we believe we need to transition from the minimum program to a maximum program. The Bolsheviks had a minimum program of their immediate actions, short-term goals, and tactical choices. But they also had a maximum program which was their long-term goals and their revolutionary transformative program: how they wanted Russia and the world to look in their Marxist-soaked imaginings. We recognize the fundamental importance of historians working with integrity (and all that entails for the nuts-and-bolts practices of research, writing, and citing), and also the importance of agreed-upon standards of professional conduct. But these, surely, are the minimum we should expect. We believe we should go further and devise a code of ethics for historians which is more ambitious, more foundational. A code of ethics should be more than just an attempt to prevent bad things from happening, or to

---

9. Read this Code of Conduct at: http://www.historytoday.com/suzannah-lipscomb/code-conduct-historians.

10. See: https://www.historians.org/jobs-and-professional-development/statements-standards-and-guidelines-of-the-discipline/statement-on-standards-of-professional-conduct.

preserve our reputation or sense of good standing in the eyes of others.[11] Most importantly, a code of ethics allows us to frame the foundational, presuppositional elements of what we do, how we do it, and why we do it. Our hope is that we can start a conversation about the calling of historians, the essence of history, and the practices that are essential to its health.

Here is ours:

A Code of Ethics

The starting point for this code of ethics is a core commitment to the universalist principle of shared human values. We make no apology for prioritizing our common humanity as something which transcends any differences we have, be they gender, race, education, class, sexuality, wealth, physical and mental well-being, ethnicity, nationality, or age. This reflects in many ways the nature of the church: an embodiment of a new way of being human, a renewed human community which has discovered something more important than its differences and seeks to live a life based on mutual trust, hospitality, and love. This sense of common humanity, however, has a temporal dimension. Because of the peculiar nature of the work of historians—we deal primarily with dead human beings, both recent and distant—this commitment to shared humanity has to extend to how we treat the dead, as well as a commitment to the work we do for humans who are currently alive, and humans who will live and die in the future.

So we argue for human solidarity as a key virtue underpinning this code of ethics. We draw heavily here upon the work of others, just adding in some of our own thoughts and ideas to give some extra flavor, color, and texture. In many ways we see this not as something chiseled onto tablets of stone, forever unchanging, but rather a living document constantly open to revision and interpretations.

The code has the following sections:

1. Historians' Responsibilities to the Living and the Dead
2. Historians' Teaching and Research: Duties and Rights
3. Historians, the Historical Profession, and the Wider Society.

---

11. To examine other codes of ethics from different groups of historians, see: http://www.concernedhistorians.org/content/ethichist.html.

Conclusion

Preamble

Historians have to take care of history. It is too important to be left neglected, too easy to abuse, and too meaningful to too many people to be left unattended. With this in mind, this code set out below provides a short summary of the duties, responsibilities, and rights of historians. As such, it is designed to be used and discussed by academic historians and all others engaged in the process of producing knowledge about the past, and should also stand as a reference point for those interested in the values and standards which guide the work of historians.

The core values which underpin this code are as follows:

- Human Solidarity
- Dignity and Respect
- Integrity
- Accountability
- History as an Act of Service

Part One: Responsibilities to the Living and the Dead

Article 1: An act of service

History is an act of service to the living and the dead. We believe that history should be carried out in pursuit of several virtues—including the promotion of human solidarity, the search for truth—and in opposition to those who wish to abuse history—to use it to deceive, distort, manipulate, or deny—or use it irresponsibly. History should never be carried out purely or primarily in ways that are self-seeking or aggrandizing, be that in the narrow sense of material or professional self-interest, or political/ideological/ethnic/cultural self-interest.

Article 2: Duties to the Dead

Historians must respect the dignity of the dead. This is a primary duty of all historians. This entails the following, which might best be encapsulated in the idea of "do unto others as you would have them do unto you":

- Treating all people equally, irrespective of how we judge or evaluate how we think they acted and behaved.

- Treating all people with respect, especially with regard to questions of privacy and their reputation. The dead have no one to advocate for them. Historians must give an even-handed account of their lives.

- Strive to make known those who have been overlooked, to give a voice to those who have been silenced, to show compassion to those who were abused.

Article 3: Duties to the Living

Historians must respect the universal rights of the living and treat them with dignity. The living constitute audiences for the work of historians. The living are the descendants of those about whom they write and carry memories and artifacts around with them. The living are also the dead to come. In this regard, historians should endeavor:

- To work with integrity and honesty (see below)
- To work with accuracy
- To present their work to others
- To pursue historical truth
- To oppose those who seek to abuse history, to deceive, or to distort

Part Two: Teaching and Research: Rights and Duties

Article 4: The Rights of Historians

Historians generally engage in two separate but related activities: research and dissemination (writing/teaching). Historians should enjoy the rights of freedom of expression, freedom to choose their field of study, and freedom to access information contained within archives and elsewhere without undue political or other types of interference when engaged in these activities.

Conclusion

Article 5: Integrity in Research and Teaching

Historians must work with integrity when they research, write, and teach. This means a set of standards (as outlined by the AHA and others) in the particulars of how historians work. These standards should include:

- Use evidence to support your interpretation and seek to understand that evidence correctly.
- Do not willfully present evidence out of context.
- Triangulate: search ardently for evidence that might undermine, as well as corroborate, your hypothesis.
- Be open to unwelcome or contradictory evidence or viewpoints or interpretations.
- Avoid assumption creep: do not allow assertions to move from possible to probably to definitely; do not build more elaborate layers of interpretation on a foundation that is rocky.
- Do not rely on the secondary assertions of other historians.
- Do not mold the facts to your interpretation.
- Root out and resolve any internal consistencies in your argument.
- Cite sources so that they can be traced, with page numbers, archival call numbers, and publication details.
- Integrity in teaching means presenting competing interpretations with fairness and intellectual honesty.
- Historians are obligated to present their credentials accurately and honestly in all contexts.
- Historians should be mindful of any *conflicts of interest* that may arise in the course of their professional duties.

Article 6: Universalism over Particularism

Historians should be sensitive to the ways in which history can be used, distorted, or manipulated for particular ends. Most notably, historians should seek to overcome the dangers of ethnocentrism, as well as others who propose a divided past.

Re-Forming History

Part Three: Historians, the Historical Profession, and the Wider Society

Historians exist in narrow professional networks as well as broader social networks. These networks create a set of responsibilities which historians need to discharge.

Article 7: Accountability, Peer Review, Self-Reflection, and Professional Autonomy

- Historians shall aspire to be as independent as possible.
- Historians shall publish and disseminate their findings as widely as possible.
- Historians shall take part willingly and fully in peer review and shall give and receive feedback as part of the normal course of their work.
- Historians shall check their findings in a free and public debate among informed and verifying colleagues.
- Historians shall be tolerant of the opinions of others.
- Historians shall reflect upon their own work and methodologies on a regular basis.
- Historians shall ensure that their profession remains autonomous and defend it against any threats to intellectual freedom.
- Historians shall display solidarity with historians and history students whose rights are under threat.

Article 8: Public Debates and Public Engagement: Curricula, Blank Spots

As part of their duty to wider society, historians should be fully engaged in the public sphere and carry out their duties as publicly as possible in the following ways:

- Historians shall seek to engage with debates in the public sphere where appropriate.
- Historians shall carry out such debates with openness, transparency, respect, and honesty.

Conclusion

- Historians shall seek to undermine any attempts by states or organizations to control the use of the past, abuse it, or manipulate it.
- Historians shall be actively involved in discussions around the content of school curricula, the focal points of public remembering, the uses of history in public spaces, and the "blank spots" or deliberate amnesia of societies.

This code hopefully expresses some of the fundamental elements of the nature of history and the responsibilities of the historian, all the way from the basic standards of integrity in historical practice, to the broad responsibilities that historians have to the living and the dead.

So, we come back to where we started. We offer our theses as the end and the beginning. A starting point for—hopefully—a long, contentious, and unsettling debate.

Back to the Beginnings . . . .

Beginnings:

95 Theses

1. History is part of creation.
2. History matters.
3. History is too important to be left unreformed.
4. "History is that impossible thing; the attempt to give an account, with incomplete knowledge, of actions themselves undertaken with incomplete knowledge."[12]
5. "History teaches us … to avoid illusion and make believe, to lay aside dreams, moonshine, cure-alls, wonder workings, pie-in-the-sky—to be realistic."[13]
6. Historians are united by a set of shared practices.
7. Historians are professional rememberers, and our disciplinary liturgies are practices of memory.
8. Historical inquiry and historical writing are recognitions of temporariness and impermanence.
9. The discipline of history is in crisis.
10. The discipline of history bears the imprint of the capitalist industrial modernity in which it exists.
11. The historical profession creates a reward structure which pushes historians to accumulate knowledge and use it for their own ends.
12. Professional history privileges white colonial narratives at the expense of stories from populations that have been suppressed and underrepresented.
13. Christian historians should start with this question: who is my neighbor?
14. There are things Christian historians should not say and stories they should not tell.

---

12. Swift, *Waterland*, 94.
13. Swift, *Waterland*, 94.

Conclusion

15. More must be said to map out distinctively Christian liturgies and approaches to history.
16. Christian historians should do antihistory.
17. Christian historians should practice dangerous remembering.
18. The Christian historian must be driven by a partisan passion for justice—past, present, and future.
19. History must serve the living and the dead.
20. We must practice knowledge as love.
21. Christian historians should work to change history as agents of healing and hope.
22. Historians must guard against tendencies toward fragmentation and overspecialization.
23. Historians must avoid reductionism, generalization, lazy stereotyping, and unwarranted speculation.
24. There exist two terrible temptations at the heart of the professional identity of historians: to exercise knowledge as power over the dead, and to use the dead to pursue our own interests and ambitions.
25. The full meaning of history is not simply in what happened, but also in what did not or could not happen.
26. It is deeply inhuman to forget the dead.
27. Christian history must be rooted in the faith of hope within history.
28. "History as told from a place of invincibility is mostly about death. History told from a place of vulnerability is mostly about life."[14]
29. Historians should listen and care before they interpret.
30. Historians should seek wisdom, not originality.
31. Historians should seek advocacy, not utility.
32. Historians should seek healing, not explanation.
33. Historians should be seekers, not finders.
34. Christian history should move beyond modernity.
35. Historians should read lovingly.

---

14. Peterson, *Christ Plays*, 151.

36. Historians should read slowly.
37. Historians should be deliberately collaborative and collegial.
38. Historical practice should be based in love, not power.
39. History is endless.
40. History should lament.
41. History should console.
42. History must confront dangerous myths.
43. History must show that nothing is permanent, fixed, immutable.
44. History must help us to resist the allure of nostalgia.
45. Historians must work for others, not themselves.
46. We should be historians *sans frontieres* in a world without borders.
47. The responsibility of the historian is to help us all to live well and faithfully in the present and to peer hopefully into the future.
48. History should contest those voices which sing the siren song of progress at the expense of tradition.
49. History is strange.
50. History should make the familiar strange and the strange familiar.
51. Christian historians should listen to strange, unmodern Christian historians.
52. The historian should be an artist, a storyteller.
53. We need to narrow the gap between history and fiction.
54. Historians must concern themselves with the textural quality of the past; what it feels like, the threads and weaves and creases.
55. Historians work with the tension of trying to recreate the past and the urge to interpret it.
56. Historians must strive for an inventiveness of form.
57. History can be a spiritual discipline.
58. History can convert us.
59. History should serve life.
60. Historians should ask this question: What do we owe the dead?

Conclusion

61. Historians should brush against the grain of history.
62. Christian history is *Hesed*.
63. Historians should remove the cloak of invisibility from the stories of the marginalized.
64. Loving-kindness and care must be extended to all.
65. Historians should make the absent present.
66. Christian historians should write counterstories.
67. Historians should know when to be silent.
68. History is not neutral.
69. Christian historians should be peacemakers.
70. Christian historians must do justice, love mercy, and walk humbly with God.
71. Christian historians should be ministers of reconciliation.
72. Historians must not play God.
73. Historians should resist all tyrannies equally.
74. Historical apologies must be accompanied by transformed social relationships.
75. There is no reconciliation without truth.
76. Storytelling and truth-telling are embedded in relationships, and some stories are not ours to tell.
77. Historians must not do epistemic injustice.
78. Historians must publicly contest those who deliberately and willfully seek to peddle lies, distortions, and half-truths about the past.
79. Christian historians should model unsettling pedagogies of history and hope.
80. Christian historians should practice Jubilee history.
81. History has always developed by both striking outward in search of the new, and looking inward to renew.
82. The historian should tend to the past with love, care, mercy, and compassion.
83. Historians must cross the border between profession and vocation.

84. Historians must cross the border between the academy and the public sphere.
85. History should not be a private conversation within the academy.
86. Historians have a significant responsibility in building human solidarity across time and space.
87. Historians must tell stories about the universality of the human experience.
88. Historians must tell stories about the differences of the human experience.
89. History must reach out to recognize historic and systemic injustices.
90. Historians must be self-reflexive.
91. Historians must honor the historical record, the fragments of the past.
92. History should seek to stir us emotionally.
93. History knows that there are endings, but no end.
94. Christian historians must be sentinels of hope against the world's forgetfulness.
95. History can show us that another world is possible.

BIBLIOGRAPHY

Appleby, Joyce, et al. *Telling the Truth about History*. New York: Norton, 1994.
Ashley, J. Matthew, ed. *A Passion for God: The Mystical-Political Dimension of Christianity*. New York: Paulist, 1998.
Atkins, Peter. *Memory and Liturgy: The Place of Memory in the Composition and Practice of Liturgy*. Brookfield, VT: Ashgate, 2004.
Atwood, Margaret. "In Search of Alias Grace." *American Historical Review* 103.5 (December 1998) 1503–16.
Bader-Saye, Scott. *Following Jesus in a Culture of Fear*. Grand Rapids: Brazos, 2007.
Bediako, Kwame. "The Doctrine of Christ and the Significance of Vernacular Terminology." *International Bulletin of Missionary Research* 22.3 (July 1998) 110–11.
Bendroth, Margaret. *The Spiritual Practice of Remembering*. Grand Rapids: Eerdmans, 2013.
Benjamin, Walter. "On the Concept of History." In *Selected Writings, Vol. 4, 1938–1940*, edited by Howard Eiland and Michael Jennings, 389–400. Translated by Edmund Jephcott et al. Cambridge, MI: The Belknap Press of Harvard University Press, 2003.
Bergen, Jeremy. *Ecclesial Repentance: The Churches Confront Their Sinful Pasts*. Edinburgh: T. & T. Clark, 2011.
Berger, John. "On the Economy of the Dead." *Harper's Magazine* (September 2008) 32.
Berger, Stefan, et al., eds. *Writing History: Theory and Practice*. London: Bloomsbury Academic, 2003.
Branch, John. "The Town of Colma, Where San Francisco's Dead Live." *New York Times* (February 5, 2016). https://www.nytimes.com/2016/02/06/sports/football/the-town-of-colma-where-san-franciscos-dead-live.html.
Brown, Callum G. *Postmodernism for Historians*. New York: Pearson Longman, 2005.
Brueggemann, Walter. *An Introduction to the Old Testament: The Canon and Christian Imagination*. Louisville: Westminster John Knox, 2003.
Burgoyne, Robert. "The Balcony of History." *Rethinking History* 11 (2007) 547–54.
Burrow, John. *A History of Histories*. London: Penguin, 2007.
Cannadine, David. *The Undivided Past*. London: Penguin, 2013.
Champion, Justin. "What are Historians for?" *Institute of Historical Research* 81 (2008) 167–88.
Christian, David. "We Need a Modern Origin Story: A Big History." *Edge* (May 21, 2015). https://www.edge.org/conversation/david_christian-we-need-a-modern-origin-story-a-big-history.

Bibliography

Cohen, Sol. "An Essay in the Aid of Writing History: Fictions of Historiography." *Studies in Philosophy and Education* 23 (2004) 317–32.
Collingwood, R. G. *The Idea of History*. Oxford: Oxford University Press, 1946.
Crockett, William R. *Eucharist: Symbol of Transformation*. New York: Pueblo, 1989.
de Baets, Antoon. "A Declaration on the Responsibilities of Present Generations toward Past Generations." *History and Theory: Studies in the Philosophy of History* 43 (2004) 130–64.
de Gruchy, John W. *Reconciliation: Restoring Justice*. Minneapolis: Fortress, 2002.
Demos, John. "In Search of Reasons for Historians to Read Novels . . ." *American Historical Review* 103 (1998) 1526–29.
Dickason, Olive. *The Myth of the Savage and the Beginnings of French Colonialism in the Americas*. Edmonton: University of Alberta Press, 1997.
Engelen, Leen. "Back to the Future, Ahead to the Past. Film and History: A Status Quaestionis." *Rethinking History* 11 (2007) 555–63.
Eusebius. *The History of the Church from Christ to Constantine*. London: Penguin, 1989.
———. *Life of Constantine the Great*. In *Nicene and Post-Nicene Fathers*. Second Series, Vol. 1, translated by Arthur Cushman McGiffert, 481–560. Grand Rapids: Eerdmans, 1991.
Evans, Richard. *Altered Pasts: Counterfactuals in History*. New York: Little, Brown, 2012.
———. *Telling Lies about Hitler*. London: Verso, 2002.
Fea, John, et al., eds. *Confessing History: Explorations in Christian Faith and the Historian's Vocation*. Notre Dame: University of Notre Dame Press, 2010.
Feldner, Heiko. "The New Scientificity in Historical Writing." In *Writing History: Theory and Practice*, edited by Stefan Berger et al., 3–21. London: Bloomsbury Academic, 2010.
Ferguson, Niall, ed. *Virtual History*. London: Picador, 1997.
Final Report of the Truth and Reconciliation Commission, Vol. 1, Summary: Honouring the Truth, Reconciling for the Future. Toronto: Lorimer, 2015. http://www.trc.ca/websites/trcinstitution/File/2015/Honouring_the_Truth_Reconciling_for_the_Future_July_23_2015.pdf.
Fisch, Jorg. "Sati and the Task of the Historian." *Journal of World History* 18 (2007) 361–68.
Furay, Conal, and Michael J. Salevouris. *The Methods and Skills of History*. Wheeling, IL: Harlan Davidson, 2010.
Gibney, Mark, et al. *The Age of Apology: Facing Up to the Past*. Philadelphia: University of Pennsylvania Press, 2008.
Gilderhus, Mark T. *History and Historians*. Englewood Cliffs, NJ: Prentice Hall, 2010.
Gorman, Jonathan. "Historians and Their Duties." *History and Theory* 43 (2004) 103–17.
Green, Anna, and Kathleen Troup. *The Houses of History*. New York: New York University Press, 1999.
Green, Jay D. *Christian Historiography: Five Rival Versions*. Waco, TX: Baylor University Press, 2016.
Grey, Mary. "A Theology for the Bearers of Dangerous Memory." In *Truth and Memory: The Church and Human Rights in El Salvador and Guatemala*, edited by Michael A. Hayes, 161–74. Leominster, UK: Gracewing, 2001.
Griffiths, Paul. *Intellectual Appetite: A Theological Grammar*. Washington, DC: Catholic University of America Press, 2009.
Harari, Yuval Noah. *Homo Deus*. New York: Signal, 2015.

Bibliography

Harink, Douglas. *Paul among the Postliberals: Pauline Theology Beyond Christendom and Modernity*. Grand Rapids: Brazos, 2003.

Hart, Jonathan. "Between History and Poetry: The Making of the Past." *Canadian Review of Comparative Literature* 29 (2002) 568–88.

Hauerwas, Stanley. *Working with Words: On Learning to Speak Christian*. Eugene, OR: Cascade, 2011.

Hauerwas, Stanley, and William H. Willimon. *Resident Aliens: Life in the Christian Colony*. Nashville: Abingdon, 1989.

Hayes, Michael A., and David Tombs, eds. *Truth and Memory: The Church and Human Rights in El Salvador and Guatemala*. Leominster, UK: Gracewing, 2001.

Heinrichs, Steve, ed. *Buffalo Shout, Salmon Cry: Conversations on Creation, Land Justice, and Life Together*. Waterloo, ON: Herald, 2013.

Herbert, Zbigniew. *Report from the Besieged City and Other Poems*. Translated with an introduction and notes by John Carpenter and Bogdana Carpenter. Oxford: Oxford University Press, 1987.

Hoefferle, Caroline. *The Essential Historiography Reader*. Boston: Prentice Hall, 2011.

Hoffer, Peter Charles. *Clio among the Muses*. New York: New York University Press, 2014.

Howard-Hassman, Rhoda E., and Mark Gibney. "Introduction: Apologies and the West." In *The Age of Apology: Facing Up to the Past*, edited by Mark Gibney et al., 1–12. Philadelphia: University of Pennsylvania Press, 2008.

Hudson, Trevor. *Discovering Our Spiritual Identity*. Downers Grove, IL: InterVarsity, 2010.

Humphreys, Melanie. "Expression of Reconciliation." Paper delivered at the TRC National Event in Edmonton, Alberta, March 30, 2014. Document in authors' possession.

Hunt, Tristram. "Reality, Identity and Empathy: The Changing Face of Social History on Television." *The Journal of Social History* 39 (2006) 843–58.

Indigenous and Northern Affairs Canada. "Statement of Apology to Former Students of Indian Residential Schools." https://www.aadnc-aandc.gc.ca/eng/1100100015644/1100100015649.

Jordanova, Ludmilla. *History in Practice*. London: Hodder Arnold, 2006.

Katerberg, William H. "Is There Such a Thing as 'Christian' History?" *Fides et Historia* 34 (2002) 57–66.

———. "The 'Objectivity Question' and the Historian's Vocation." In *Confessing History: Explorations in Christian Faith and the Historian's Vocation*, edited by John Fea, et al., 101–27. Notre Dame: University of Notre Dame Press, 2010.

———. "The Person of the Historian." *Fides et Historia* 44 (2012) 76–81.

Kennedy, Rick. "Introduction: The Sacred Calling of History." *Fides et Historia* 35 (2003) 1–6.

Kidd, Ian James, et al., eds. *The Routledge Handbook of Epistemic Injustice*. London: Routledge, 2017.

King, Martin Luther, Jr. "Letter From Birmingham Jail (August 1963)." https://web.cn.edu/kwheeler/documents/Letter_Birmingham_Jail.pdf.

King, Thomas. *The Inconvenient Indian*. London: Penguin, 2013.

Koster, Wendelin. "Recovering Collective Memory in the Context of Postmodernism." In *Liturgy in a Postmodern World*, edited by Keith F. Pecklers, 32–35. New York: Continuum, 2003.

Lambert, Peter. "The Professionalization and Institutionalization of History." In *Writing History: Theory and Practice*, edited by Stefan Berger et al., 40–58. London: Bloomsbury, 2010.

Bibliography

Lane, Dermot. "Memory in the Service of Reconciliation and Hope." In *Truth and Memory: The Church and Human Rights in El Salvador and Guatemala*, edited by Michael A. Hayes, 175-93. Leominster, UK: Gracewing, 2001.

Lemon, M.C. "The Structure of Narrative." In *The History and Narrative Reader*, edited by Geoffrey Roberts, 107-29. London: Routledge, 2001.

Leuchtenburg, William E. "Presidential Address: The Historian and the Public Realm." *American Historical Review* 97 (1992) 1-18.

Link, Arthur S. "The Historian's Vocation." In *God, History and Historians*, edited by C. T. McIntire, 373-89. New York: Oxford University Press, 1977.

Lipstadt, Deborah. *Denying the Holocaust: the Growing Assault on Truth and Memory*. London: Penguin, 1994.

———. *History on Trial*. New York: Harper, 2005.

Longxi, Zhang. "History and Fictionality: Insights and Limitations of a Literary Perspective." *Rethinking History* 8 (2004) 387-402.

Louth, Andrew. "Introduction." In *Eusebius: History of the Christian Church*, edited by Andrew Louth, ix-xiii. New York: Penguin, 1989.

Lowenthal, David. *The Past is a Foreign Country [Revisited]*. Cambridge, UK: Cambridge University Press, 2015.

Lowman, Emma Battell, and Adam J. Barker. *Settler: Identity and Colonialism in 21st Century Canada*. Halifax, NS: Fernwood, 2015.

Lyons, Matthew. "Between Fact and Fiction." *History Today* 66 (2016) 46.

Marsden, George, and Frank Roberts, eds. *A Christian View of History?* Grand Rapids: Eerdmans, 1975.

———. "Common Sense and the Spiritual Vision of History." In *History and Historical Understanding*, edited by C. T. McIntire, and R. A. Wells, 55-68. Grand Rapids: Eerdmans, 1984.

———. *The Outrageous Idea of Christian Scholarship*. New York: Oxford University Press, 1997.

———. "What Difference Might Christian Perspectives Make?" In *History and the Christian Historian*, edited by Ronald A. Wells, 11-22. Grand Rapids: Eerdmans, 1998.

Marwick, Arthur. *The New Nature of History*. Houndmills, UK: Palgrave, 2001.

McCarraher, Eugene. "On a Certain Blindness in Historians." *Fides et Historia* 44 (2012) 54-60.

McGiffert, Arthur Cushman, ed. *Nicene and Post-Nicene Fathers*. Second Series, Vol. 1. New York: The Christian Literature Company, 1890.

McIntire, C. T., ed. *God, History and Historians*. New York: OUP, 1977.

McIntire, C. T., and R. A. Wells, eds. *History and Historical Understanding*. Grand Rapids: Eerdmans, 1984.

Merton, Thomas. *No Man is an Island*. Boston: Shambala, 2005.

Metz, Johann Baptist. *The Emergent Church: The Future of Christianity in a Post-bourgeois World*. Translated by Peter Mann. New York: Crossroads, 1987.

———. *Faith in History and Society: Toward a Practical Fundamental Theology*. New York: Seabury, 1980.

———. "The Future in the Memory of Suffering." In *Faith and the Future: Essays on Theology, Solidarity, and Modernity*, edited by Johann Metz and Juergen Moltmann, 100-118. Maryknoll, NY: Orbis, 1995.

Bibliography

———. "On the Biographical Itinerary of My Theology." In *A Passion for God: The Mystical-Political Dimension of Christianity*, edited by J. Matthew Ashley, 1–6. New York: Paulist, 1998.

Middleton, J. Richard, and Brian J. Walsh. *Truth is Stranger than it Used to Be: Biblical Faith in a Postmodern Age*. Downers Grove, IL: InterVarsity, 1995.

Morrill, Bruce T. *Anamnesis as Dangerous Memory: Political and Liturgical Theology in Dialogue*. Collegeville, MN: Liturgical, 2000.

Mosse, George. *On the Occasion of his Retirement. 17.6.85*. Jerusalem: Hebrew University of Jerusalem, 1986.

Munslow, Alan. *The New History*. Harlow, UK: Pearson, 2003.

Nabokov, Vladimir. *Speak, Memory: An Autobiography Revisited*. New York: Vintage, 1951.

Niezen, Ronald. *Truth and Indignation: Canada's Truth and Reconciliation Commission on Indian Residential Schools*. Toronto: University of Toronto Press, 2013.

Nietzsche, Friedrich *Untimely Meditations*. Edited by Daniel Breazeale. Translated by R. J. Hollingdale. Cambridge, UK: Cambridge University Press, 1997.

O'Brien, Tim. *The Things They Carried*. Boston: Mariner, 1990.

Pecklers, Keith, ed. *Liturgy in a Postmodern World*. New York: Continuum, 2003.

Peterson, Eugene. *Christ Plays in Ten Thousand Places*. Grand Rapids: Eerdmans, 2005.

———. *Eat This Book*. Grand Rapids: Eerdmans, 2009.

Pouncy, Carolyn J. "History, Real and Invented." *Kritika: Explorations in Russian and Eurasian History* 15 (2014) 343–52.

Ranciere, Jacques. *The Names of History*. Minneapolis: University of Minnesota Press, 1994.

Regan, Paulette. *Unsettling the Settler Within: Indian Residential Schools, Truth Telling, and Reconciliation in Canada*. Vancouver: University of British Columbia Press, 2010.

Roberts, Geoffrey, ed. *The History and Narrative Reader*. London: Routledge, 2001.

Rosenstone, Robert. *History on Film/Film on History*. Harlow, UK: Pearson, 2012.

Rozett, Robert. "Gathering the Fragments." *The Jerusalem Post* (May 1, 2011). http://www.jpost.com/Opinion/Op-Ed-Contributors/Gathering-the-fragments.

Rusen, Jorn. "How to Overcome Ethnocentrism: Approaches to a Culture of Recognition by History in the Twenty-First Century." *History and Theory* 43 (2004) 118–29.

Russell, Jeffrey B. "Glory in Time: the Longing of the Cosmos to Return to God." *Soundings* 22 (1991) 41–58.

Ryan, Barbara. Review of *Damaged Identities*, by Hilda Lineman Nelson and *Women Escaping Violence: Empowerment Through Narrative*, by Elaine J. Lawless. *NWSA Journal* 16.2 (2004) 234–37.

Sakenfeld, Katharine. *The Meaning of Hesed in the Hebrew Bible: A New Inquiry*. Missoula, MT: Scholars, 1978.

Sandle, Mark, and William Van Arragon. "Toward a Practice of Christian Antihistory: Writing the Antihistory of Soviet Communism." *Fides et Historia* 46.2 (Summer/Fall 2014) 85–99.

Schama, Simon. *Dead Certainties*. London: Granta, 1991.

Schuster, Ekkehard, and Reinhold Boschert-Kimmig, eds. *Hope against Hope: Johann Baptist Metz and Elie Wiesel Speak Out on the Holocaust*. Translated by J. Matthew Ashley. New York: Paulist, 1999.

Bibliography

Schweiger, Beth Barton. "Seeing Things: Knowledge and Love in History." In *Confessing History: Explorations in Christian Faith and the Historian's Vocation*, edited by John Fea et al., 60–82. Notre Dame: University of Notre Dame Press, 2010.

Simon, Julius, ed. *History, Religion and Meaning: American Reflections on the Holocaust and Israel*. Westport, CT: Greenwood, 2000.

Smith, James. *Imagining the Kingdom: How Worship Works*. Grand Rapids: Baker Academic, 2013.

Smith, Linda Tuhiwai. *Decolonizing Methodologies: Research and Indigenous Peoples*. London: Zed, 2012.

Spiegel, Gabrielle M. "Presidential Address: The Task of the Historian." *American Historical Review* 114 (2009) 1–15.

Steedman, Carolyn. "About Ends: On How the End is Different from an Ending." *History of the Human Sciences* 9 (1996) 99–114.

———. *Dust*. Manchester, UK: Manchester University Press, 2001.

Stephenson, Wesley. "Do the Dead Outnumber the Living?" *BBC News* (February 4, 2012). https://www.bbc.com/news/magazine-16870579.

Stewart, Michael. "Harper's Franklin 'Discovery': Or, Did Anyone Ask the Inuit?" *Rabble* (September 9, 2014). http://rabble.ca/blogs/bloggers/michael-stewart/2014/09/harpers-franklin-discovery-or-did-anyone-ask-inuit.

Storey, William Kelleher, and Towser Jones. *Writing History*. Don Mills, ON: Oxford University Press Canada, 2011.

Suderman, W. Derek. "Reflections of a Christian Settler in the Haldimand Tract." In *Buffalo Shout, Salmon Cry: Conversations on Creation, Land Justice, and Life Together*, edited by Steve Heinrichs, 263–77. Waterloo, ON: Herald, 2013.

Sweeney, Douglas. "On the Vocation of Historians to the Priesthood of Believers: Faithful Practices in Service of the Guild." *Fides et Historia* 39 (2007) 1–13.

Swift, Graham. *Waterland*. London: Picador, 1984.

Tosh, John. *The Pursuit of History*. London: Routledge: 2006.

Truth and Reconciliation Commission of Canada. *Final Report of the Truth and Reconciliation Commission, Vol. 1, Summary: Honouring the Truth, Reconciling for the Future*. Toronto: Lorimer, 2015.

Tsosie, Rebecca. "Indigenous Peoples, Anthropology, and the Legacy of Epistemic Injustice." In *The Routledge Handbook of Epistemic Injustice*, edited by Ian James Kidd et al., 356–69. New York: Routledge, 2017.

Tuchman, Barbara. *Practicing History*. New York: Ballantine, 1982.

Van Arragon, William. "People of Hope, People of Memory: Theologies of Memory and the Christian Historian." *Fides et Historia* 37:2 (Summer 2005); 38:1 (Spring 2006) 41–49.

Van Dam, Raymond. *Remembering Constantine at the Milvian Bridge*. New York: Cambridge University Press, 2011.

Wells, Ronald A. "Beyond 'Religious History': The Calling of the Christian Historian." *Fides et Historia* 34 (2002) 41–47.

Wells, Ronald A., ed. *History and the Christian Historian*. Grand Rapids: Eerdmans, 1998.

White, Hayden. "Foreword." In *The Names of History*, by Jacques Ranciere, vii–xix. Minneapolis: University of Minnesota Press, 1994.

———. "Historiography and Historiophoty." *American Historical Review* 93 (1988) 1193–99.

Bibliography

Williams, Rowan. *A Ray of Darkness: Sermons and Reflections*. Cambridge, MA: Cowley, 1995.

———. *Why Study the Past? The Quest for the Historical Church*. Grand Rapids: Eerdmans, 2005.

Wilson, Shaun. *Research is Ceremony: Indigenous Research Methods*. Black Point, NS: Fernwood, 2008.

Woolf, Nicky. "Canada Uses Franklin Expedition Wreck to Boost North-West Passage Claim." *The Guardian* (September 13, 2014). http://www.theguardian.com/world/2014/sep/13/canada-uses-franklin-expedition-wreck-north-west-passage-claim.

Wyschogrod, Edith. "The Shoah and the Historian's Passion for the Dead Others." In *History, Religion and Meaning: American Reflections on the Holocaust and Israel*, edited by Julius Simon, 27–38. Westport, CT: Greenwood, 2000.

NAME/SUBJECT INDEX

A

Aetna, 120
Africa, 31, 96,
American Historical Association (AHA), 22, 155, 159
Anglican Church (Canada), 128
Annales School, 32
Antihistory, 2, 18, 39, 40, 42, 44, 47, 49, 118, 119, 130, 163
Apology (-ies), 5, 115, 116, 117, 119, 120, 121, 123, 128, 129, 130, 131, 140, 165
archive (s), 10, 30, 33, 37, 52, 53, 55, 63, 91, 93, 97, 98, 111, 114, 121, 129, 135, 141, 150, 153, 158,
Ataturk, Kemal, 109
Atkins, Peter, 48
Atwood, Margaret, 86
Augustine, St., 50, 74
Auschwitz, 41

B

Bader-Saye, Scott, 76–77
Barker, Adam J., 124
Bediako, Kwame, 13, 13n15
Benjamin, Walter, 42, 46, 98
Bergen, Jeremy, 120, 121, 130
Berger, John, 106, 107n31
Bible, 107
biblical, 66, 72–73
"Big History," 74–75

Black Death, 96
Bolshevik Party, 155
Bonhoeffer, Dietrich, 41
Book of Common Prayer, 119
Bunting, Heinrich (map), 49–50

C

Canadian Historical Association, 22
Champion, Justin, 64, 66,
Christ, 3n3, 13, 13n15, 17, 18, 42, 43, 45, 46, 48–51, 69, 71, 73, 76, 77, 121, 122, 152, 163n14
Christian, David, 74–75
Christianity, 43
church, 6, 7, 8, 11, 17, 18, 41n7, 42–43, 45, 47, 48, 50, 51, 68–71, 73, 77, 115, 116, 117, 119, 121, 122, 127, 127–131, 143, 156
Churchill, Winston, 109
Clio, 72
Cohen, Sol, 87
Collingwood, R.G., 74
Colma, 95
Colonialism, 45, 118, 121, 124, 125, 126, 127, 128, 130, 135, 137, 141, 142
Conference on Faith and History, 15
Conference on US Intellectual History, 14
Constantine, 68–69, 70–71, 78
constructionists, 34–35,
counterfactuality, 83

Name/Subject Index

Crockett, William, 48
curiosity, 8, 58, 62, 64, 90, 133, 145, 147, 149,
curricula, 150, 160, 161

D

Dangerous memory, 18, 40, 42–49, 118, 119, 130, 132
De Baets, Antoine, 99–101 153n8
deconstructionists, 34–35,
de Gruchy, John, 118, 122, 123, 124, 139
Demos, John, 86
Dickason, Olive, 126
Doctrine of Discovery, 126, 127, 136, 141
documentaries, 25, 81
Dumont, Marilyn, 136

E

empathy, 16, 24, 35, 46, 47, 55, 58, 62, 81, 82, 87, 132,
empirical, 28–30, 33, 34, 35, 38, 70,
Enlightenment, 28, 50, 74, 79,
Epistemic injustice, 136
ethics, 16, 19, 22, 46, 48, 99, 154–56
ethnocentrism, 152, 152n6&7, 159
Eucharist, 18, 42, 43, 45, 48, 51,
Eusebius, 68, 70–74

F

Fides et Historia, 15
France, 31, 98, 110
Franklin Expedition, 134–37
French, 12, 98, 111
Fiction, 84–87
films, 8, 27, 81, 82, 86

G

Gerardi, Juan, 46
German School, 29,
Georgetown University, 120–21
globalization, 151

God, 4, 5, 13, 14, 16, 17, 19, 23, 28, 41–51, 62, 68, 72, 73–77, 85, 102, 103, 107, 117, 120, 121, 122, 123, 134, 145, 146, 152, 165
gods, 68, 71, 72
Good Samaritan, 145–47
Green, Anna, 29,
Green, Jay, 16–17,
Grey, Mary, 46–47
Griffiths, Paul, 64

H

Harper, Stephen, 115, 116, 123, 129, 130, 134, 137n29
Herbert, Zbigniew, 107
Herodotus, 71, 78
hesed, 4, 19, 89, 101–5, 107–10, 112, 113, 114, 118, 165
historia, 79
Historian (s), Christian, vii, 2, 5, 6, 11–19, 23, 39, 40, 42, 44, 45, 47, 50, 51, 53, 67, 69, 74, 75, 78, 97, 117–18, 123, 130, 138, 140, 143, 144–46, 152, 162–66
history academic 27, 65, 81, 85, 87,
and fiction, 84–87
modernist 38, 43, 65, 68, 148,
popular, 27
scientific, 30
Holocaust, 41, 101, 106, 111, 120
humility, 17, 47, 55, 62, 63, 65, 91, 129, 131,

I

incarnational, 18, 43, 45, 51, 53, 55, 146,
Indian Act, 127
Indian Residential Schools Settlement Agreement, 129
Indigenous research methodologies, 137–38
individualism, 53, 60, 148

Name/Subject Index

Irving, David, 101

J

Jesus, 47, 51, 76n17–19, 77, 139, 145, 146, 147
Jewish, 19, 102, 111
Jews, 41, 111
Jordanova, Ludmilla, 10, 21, 59, 169
Jubilee, 5, 142, 143, 165
Judenplatz, 106

K

Katerberg, William, 17, 23, 24, 39, 65, 66, 92, 153
King Jr., Martin Luther, 148
King, Thomas, 125
Koster, Wendelin, 48

L

Lane, Dermot, 46–47
Lenin, Vladimir Ilych, 109
Lipscomb, Suzannah, 155
Lipstadt, Deborah, 101–2
Littlechild, Wilton, 116
liturgies, 2, 10, 11, 13, 14, 21, 28, 31, 39, 41, 51, 65, 67, 117, 118, 123, 130, 132, 136, 139, 143, 144, 162, 163,
Lowenthal, David, 28, 31,
Lowman, Emma Battell, 124
Luther, Martin, 1, 6, 7

M

Marsden, George, 15–16
Marxism (t), 32, 43, 80, 155,
Merton, Thomas, 62,
Metz, Johann Baptist, 18, 39–51, 68, 93, 98, 118, 130, 132
Michelet, Jules, 98
modernist, 38, 41, 43, 45, 53, 54, 55, 59, 65, 68, 118, 135, 139, 144, 148,

modernity, 2, 3, 13, 14, 24, 38, 44, 50, 54, 57, 59–60, 67, 73, 75, 106, 107, 144, 162, 163
Moldavia, 92–93
Mosse, George, 77–78
Mr. Cogito on the Need for Precision, 107
Murray, Sinclair, 116, 143
Museum (s), 81, 141, 150

N

Nanking, Rape of, 146,
National Centre for Truth and Reconciliation, 129
nationalism, 130, 134, 151
Nazi, 27, 40, 110, 125, 147
Nazism, 111
neoliberalism, 61,
Newton, Isaac, 60,
Niezen, Ronald, 132, 133,
nostalgia, 3, 107, 164
Novels, historical, 8, 81, 84, 86

O

O'Brien, Tim, 84, 85n37, 112
objectivity, 13, 15, 17, 23–24, 30, 31, 53, 56, 65–66, 77, 78, 132, 137, 148,
Oradour sur Glane, 110–11
Ossario di San Martino, 96,

P

Peterson, Eugene, 3n3, 48, 49n32, 58
postmodern, (-ism, -ity) 8, 11, 12, 13, 23, 29, 34, 40, 45, 63, 92,
post-structuralism, 12
Presbyterian Church of Canada, 128
professionalization, 19, 27, 30, 31, 32, 38, 144,
Providence (providentialism), 14, 17, 72, 74–76, 78, 139

Name/Subject Index

R

Rabe, John, 147
Ranciere, Jacques, 98,
Reconciliation, 5, 18, 19, 43, 46, 47, 49, 115–26, 128–35, 139–42, 165
reconstructionists, 34–35
reenactment, 82–83
Regan, Paulette, 131, 132, 141–42
Reformation, 6, 7, 8, 12, 28, 122
Residential schools,
    Canada's apology for, 115–17
    Canada's history of, 123–29
    and genocide, 115, 125–26
resurrection, 42, 43, 48, 50, 51, 73, 76, 98
Robespierre, Maximilien, 109
Romania, 92–93
Romero, Oscar, 46
Rosenstone, Robert, 86
Rusen, Jorn, 152
Russell, Jeffrey, 94,
Russia, 155

S

sacred, 13, 14, 39–41, 44, 54, 56–58, 74, 131
Sakenfeld, Katherine Doob, 103,
San Francisco, 95,
science, 23, 28, 29, 46, 75,
    natural, 23, 74, 75,
    social, 22, 35,
scientific revolution, 28,
Schweiger, Beth Barton, 62, 97, 114, 147,
Settlers, 124–25, 126, 130, 132, 141, 142
Shoah, 99, 111
Smith, Linda Tuhiwai, 137–38
Smith, James K., 11, 11n9&11
Social media, 81, 150
solidarity, 5, 18, 46, 54, 65, 101, 148, 151, 152, 156, 157, 160, 166
sources, 12, 25, 30, 32, 33, 34, 36, 56, 61, 73, 86, 140, 159
    primary, 29, 30, 33, 36, 71, 135, secondary, 29, 35,
South Africa, 120, 122
Steedman, Carolyn, 10, 10n 7&8, 11, 11n10, 84n36, 86, 87n44, 98n13&15&16, 144n1, 172
Suderman, W. Derek, 142
Swift, Graham, 1n1, 2n2, 6n4, 9, 9n5, 67n1&2, 105, 106n30, 162n12&13,

T

Tamerlane, 109
Thatcher, Margaret, 109
The Things They Carried, 84, 85n37, 112,
Thucydides, 71, 79
Tosh, John, 36n20, 78, 80n28&29, 139
Troup, Kathleen, 29,
truth, 5, 12, 12n12, 23, 28–30, 32, 33, 36, 43, 46n21, 52, 55, 56, 59–61, 63, 65, 71, 73, 76, 78, 79, 84, 85, 90, 101, 105, 107, 112, 113, 116, 119, 122, 126, 129–32, 146, 148, 150, 153, 154, 157, 165
    happening, 84, 85
    historical 11, 12, 24, 28, 133, 158
    story, 84, 85
    telling, 5, 17, 24, 28, 133, 158
Truth and Reconciliation Commission of Canada (TRC), 19, 116–43
    Activities, 129–30
    Calls to Action, 140–41
    Commissioners of, 116
    Final Report, 125
    National Event, 116, 130–31,
    Survivors' Testimony, 131–33
Tuchman, Barbara, 78
turn,
    cultural, 12
    linguistic, 12, 24,
    liturgical, 11
    theological, 7, 13, 14, 54, 121

Name/Subject Index

U

United Church of Canada, 128
Utopia (s), 43, 51, 146

V

Video games, 81, 83
Vietnam, 84, 112
vocation, 5, 8, 13, 17, 18, 65, 90, 121, 139, 140, 143, 146, 149, 165

W

Waterland, 1n1, 2n2, 6n4, 9, 9n5, 67n172, 105, 106n30, 162n12713

Whiteread, Rachel, 106
Williams, Rowan, 50–51, 69, 97
Wilson, Marie, 116
wisdom, 3, 14, 28, 47, 54, 56, 57, 58, 61, 66, 96, 114, 129, 149, 163
World War 1, 80, 109
World War Two, 32, 92, 93
Wyschogrod, Edyth, 99

Y

Yad Vesham, 111

Z

Zinn, Howard, 65, 66

SCRIPTURE INDEX

OLD TESTAMENT

Genesis
47: 29–30   102 n28

Proverbs
31:8   146

NEW TESTAMENT

Matthew
10:16   56 n1

www.ingramcontent.com/pod-product-compliance
Lightning Source LLC
Chambersburg PA
CBHW020849160426
43192CB00007B/848